United States
Department
of Agriculture

Forest Service

**Rocky Mountain
Research Station**

General Technical
Report RMRS-GTR-145

March 2005

Stereo Photo Guide for Estimating Canopy Fuel Characteristics in Conifer Stands

Joe H. Scott
Elizabeth D. Reinhardt

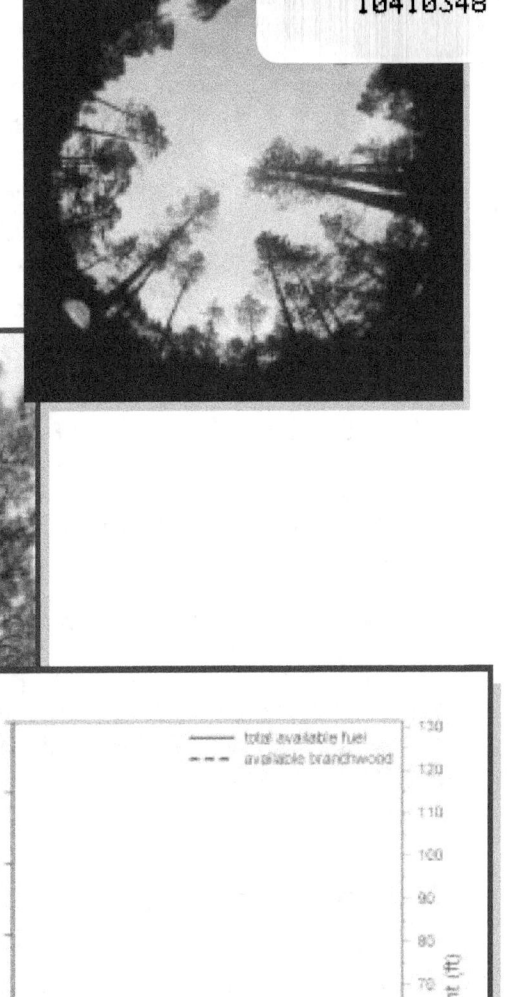

Abstract

Scott, Joe H.; Reinhardt, Elizabeth D. 2005. **Stereo photo guide for estimating canopy fuel characteristics in conifer stands**. Gen. Tech. Rep. RMRS-GTR-145. Fort Collins, CO: U.S. Department of Agriculture, Forest Service, Rocky Mountain Research Station. 49 p. plus stereoscope.

Stereo photographs, hemispherical photographs, and stand data are presented with associated biomass and canopy fuel characteristics for five Interior West conifer stands. Canopy bulk density, canopy base height, canopy biomass by component, available canopy fuel load, and vertical distribution of canopy fuel are presented for each plot at several stages of sampling, each corresponding to a level of simulated low thinning (100, 75, 50, and 25 percent of the initial basal area). This guide will help fuel managers estimate canopy fuel characteristics in similar forest conditions.

Keywords: canopy bulk density, canopy biomass, canopy base height, ponderosa pine, Douglas-fir, lodgepole pine, Sierra Nevada mixed conifer

The Authors

Joe H. Scott has been a Research Forester with Systems for Environmental Management, a nonprofit research and education foundation in Missoula, MT, since 1996. He has conducted investigations related to surface and canopy fuel characteristics, fire behavior modeling, and crown fire hazard assessment. From 1990 to 1996 he held positions as Forestry Specialist at University of California at Berkeley, Research Technician at the Intermountain Research Station's Fire Sciences Laboratory in Missoula, and Consulting Forester and Logger specializing in residential forestry in Missoula. Joe earned a B.S. degree in forestry and resource management from the University of California at Berkeley and an M.S. degree in forestry from the University of Montana, Missoula.

Elizabeth D. Reinhardt is a Research Forester in the Prescribed Fire and Fire Effects Project at the Rocky Mountain Research Station, Fire Sciences Laboratory, Missoula, MT. She has degrees in English (A.B., Harvard University) and forestry (M.S. 1982, and Ph.D., 1991, University of Montana). Her research has included studies of tree mortality, fuel consumption, modeling fire effects, and canopy fuels. She has worked on the development of FOFEM, FFE-FVS, and FuelCalc.

Acknowledgments

This work was funded by the Joint Fire Science Program, U.S. Department of Agriculture, and U.S. Department of the Interior, and supported by the USDA Forest Service Rocky Mountain Research Station and Systems for Environmental Management. We thank Steve Slaughter and Laura Ward, Ninemile Ranger District, Lolo National Forest; Terry Hershey, Salmon-Cobalt Ranger District, and Barb Levesque, Salmon-Challis National Forest; Allen Farnsworth and Chuck McHugh, Coconino National Forest; Bob Heald, Jason Moghaddas, Frieder Schurr, and Sheryl Rambeau, University of California, Center for Forestry, Blodgett Forest Research Station; and Ward McCaughey and Leon Theroux, Rocky Mountain Research Station's Missoula Forestry Sciences Laboratory for facilitating field work. We also thank the field crew members Kylie Kramer, Matthew Duveneck, Dustin Walters, Bill Ballinger, Niki Parenteau, Andrew Christie, and Roham Abtahi. We are grateful to Olga Helmy for processing the photographs, and to Kathy Gray for data analysis and summary. We are grateful to Roger Ottmar, Pacific Northwest Research Station, and Robert Ziel, Michigan Department of Natural Resources, for their helpful comments on this manuscript.

Stereo Photo Guide for Estimating Canopy Fuel Characteristics in Conifer Stands

Joe H. Scott
Elizabeth D. Reinhardt

Introduction _____

Crown fires in conifer forests are a concern to forest managers in the Western United States; they have, for a variety of reasons, increased in frequency and extent in many forest types (Arno and Brown 1991; Mutch and others 1993). Compared to surface fires, crown fires exhibit higher spread rate and flame length, leading to many more burned acres (per unit time), more smoke per acre, greater and longer lasting ecological effects (higher severity), greater threats to firefighter and public safety, and increased risk of property loss. Private and government land managers need to identify areas with high potential for crown fire, and to design fuel treatments that reduce the potential for crown fire.

Research over the last few decades has shown a number of canopy fuel characteristics to directly or indirectly affect the incidence and behavior of crown fires (Agee 1996; Albini and Baughman 1979; Fahnestock 1970; Rothermel 1991; Scott 1998; Van Wagner 1977):

- canopy base height—distance from the ground surface to the base of the canopy fuel stratum

- canopy bulk density—mass of available canopy fuel per unit canopy volume

- canopy fuel load—the mass of available canopy fuel per unit ground area

- stand height—average height of the tallest trees in a stand

- canopy cover—percent of vertically projected canopy cover in the stand

- foliar moisture content—moisture content of conifer foliage

A number of tabular and mathematical fire models and computer-based fire modeling systems require estimates of these canopy fuel characteristics for simulating crown fire hazard (Fahnestock 1970; Kilgore and Sando 1975; Scott and Reinhardt 2001), behavior (Cruz 1999; Finney 1998; Rothermel 1991), or effects (Reinhardt and others 1997). This photo guide includes estimates of all canopy fuel characteristics mentioned above except foliar moisture content, which varies seasonally (Philpot and Mutch 1971). More information on estimating foliar moisture content can be found in Alexander (1988) and Scott and Reinhardt (2001).

We measured canopy fuels on a single fixed-radius plot at each of five study sites in the Interior West, each in a different conifer forest type. Each plot required approximately 1,000 person-hours to complete all sampling. The forest types and sites sampled included:

- ponderosa pine/Douglas-fir (PPDF)—Lolo National Forest, near Missoula, Montana

- lodgepole pine stand (LP)—Tenderfoot Experimental Forest, north-central Montana

- Douglas-fir/lodgepole pine (DFLP)—Salmon-Challis National Forest, near Salmon, Idaho

- ponderosa pine (PP)—Coconino National Forest, near Flagstaff, Arizona

- Sierra Nevada Mixed Conifer (SNMC)—Blodgett Forest Research Station, Center for Forestry, University of California, Berkeley, near Auburn, California

This photo guide is part of a larger canopy fuels project; study site selection and exact plot location was guided by the needs of the project as a whole. Plot locations were not chosen randomly, but instead with the goal of including specific stand structures. For example, the PP plot near Flagstaff was in the densest portion of the densest stand available to us; it does not characterize PP stands in general or even those nearby—it was chosen to test the use of existing allometric equations to estimate canopy fuel characteristics at an abnormally high stand density.

With only one site in each forest type and only one plot at each site, these values must not to be used as estimates for the forest type in general, or even for the study site. Further study is needed to draw conclusions about canopy characteristics in various forest types.

How to Use This Guide _____

This photo guide is not extensive enough to be used reliably in all conifer forest types. However, accurate information on canopy characteristics is so lacking (and needed) that even this limited-extent guide may prove useful in calibrating our eyes to "see" canopy characteristics such as canopy bulk density and canopy fuel load. This guide does not contain enough data points to be used as the sole basis for estimating canopy characteristics in the field.

We recommend you read the entire text of this paper in order to understand how the data was collected or estimated, and what each piece of information means. The "Anatomy of a Guide Page" section is particularly useful for that purpose.

Next, using a commercially available pocket stereoscope (or the hand-held stereoscope provided), examine the stereo photos and data for each fully stocked plot (that is, before any trees had been removed for sampling). This will give you an idea of the range of initial conditions covered in the guide. Note the visual density of foliage and fine branchwood in the photos, and relate that to the tabulated canopy fuel characteristics and canopy fuel profile. Visually compare the stereo images with a fully stocked stand as you walk through it to roughly estimate its canopy fuel characteristics.

We do not wish to imply that the densest plot in this guide is necessarily the upper limit on canopy characteristics of all stands in all forest types. Canopy characteristics may be more dense than we observed on these plots, even within one of our sampled forest types.

Finally, examine the series of guide pages for each site at different sampling stages and associate those visual images with the canopy fuel data provided. This offers an idea of how canopy fuels changed as tree density was reduced by progressively removing trees, smaller diameters first. The sampling stages were designed to roughly simulate a thinning from below in increments of 25 percent of the initial basal area. Other "treatments" could have very different effects on canopy fuels, even if the residual basal area is the same as in our study.

Because of the significant influence of stand density on tree growth and canopy architecture, our sampling stages do not necessarily reflect canopy fuel characteristics of unmanaged stands at one of the residual basal area levels in our study. For example, we should not expect that an unmanaged stand with 100 ft^2 per acre of basal area necessarily has the same characteristics as a stand that was thinned to the same basal area from a denser initial condition.

Sampling Method

At each study site we installed a single fixed-radius plot. Plot radius was 10 m except at the PPDF and SNMC sites, which were 15-m-radius plots (due to their lower stem density). At each plot we mapped and measured basic characteristics of every tree: species, diameter at breast height, crown position, tree height, and crown base height. Before beginning destructive sampling, we made stereo photographs of the plot and captured digital hemispherical images from a 25-point grid (5-m spacing) centered at plot center.

We conducted the sampling in stages, beginning with the smallest diameter trees in each plot and working toward the larger diameter trees. When we had sampled 25 percent of the initial basal area, we rephotographed the plot (stereo and hemispherical). This guide contains photos and data for the fully stocked stand, as well as with 25, 50, and 75 percent of the

basal area removed. This method provided estimates of canopy fuel characteristics as if the stand had received thinning from below treatments of increasing intensity. This sampling method is not an exact simulation of thinning from below, because the trees were sampled strictly based on diameter with no regard given to tree vigor or residual spacing.

The PPDF and SNMC study sites had a significant understory tree component. In those plots we added an additional sampling stage, roughly corresponding to an understory removal treatment, in which we first removed the understory trees (less than 5 cm d.b.h. in the PPDF stand; less than 15 cm d.b.h. in the SNMC stand). The remaining stages were as described above.

For each sample tree, we weighed every branch at least 1 cm diameter and recorded its height above the ground, basal diameter, and length. We sorted a systematic subsample of branches into size classes (by cutting each branch at breakpoint diameters) and components (live versus dead) to obtain weight of live foliage, live branchwood (by diameter class), cones, dead branchwood (by diameter class), and lichen and moss. We used the following diameter class breakpoints in sorting subsample branches:

- 0 to 3 mm diameter
- 3 to 6 mm diameter
- 6 to 10 mm diameter
- 10 to 25 mm diameter
- 25 to 50 mm diameter
- 50+ mm diameter

A subset of the sorted material was oven dried to determine moisture content. Using corrected dry-weight data for the sorted branches, we developed regression equations to estimate the oven-dry weight of foliage and branchwood by size class for every branch on every tree.

We summarized the individual-tree data to the plot level in 1-m vertical layers. This guide focuses on the available canopy fuel, which is only a portion of the total canopy biomass we measured. Available canopy fuel is estimated here as the live foliage plus the live 0- to 3-mm-diameter class and dead 0- to 6-mm-diameter class biomass. Larger size classes of both live and dead canopy biomass do not burn in the short period of time of flaming during a crown fire (less than 1 minute); therefore, they are not included as available canopy fuel.

Although certainly not related to crown fire or canopy fuels, we also measured diameter of the bole at various heights in order to estimate bole volume and mass. This information will be used later to estimate the potential harvest volume of alternative canopy fuel treatments applied to each stand.

Anatomy of a Guide Page Pair

This publication contains 22 guide page pairs, one for each site at each stage of sampling, plus an extra guide page pair corresponding to understory removal stages for the SNMC and PPDF sites. This section describes the information shown on each guide page pair, including a description of how each piece of information was compiled.

Stereo Photo Pair

Before each sampling stage we made several exposures of slide film using a 35 mm camera and tripod placed approximately 15 m from plot center; the immediate foreground of the photos is therefore outside the plot. Stereo pairs were made by simply moving the camera and tripod approximately 8 inches (tangential to plot center), recomposing, and making several more exposures. (We now use a simple, inexpensive tool to assist in making co-registered stereo images.) Because photographing the plot before each stage was a necessary step before continuing field sampling, we could not afford to wait for optimal light conditions. Most photographs were made in the early morning hours. As a result, many of the images were of poor quality; either the bright highlights were overexposed, or the darker shadows were black. The human eye can sense a much wider range of light intensity than can be captured digitally or on film.

We scanned our slides and used digital imaging techniques to improve the images. Each slide was scanned twice, once normally and again with the scanner "analog gain" set to its highest position. (In some cases we scanned two separate slides of differing exposures, then manually co-registered them.) Using professional photo processing software we composited the two images into a single, more evenly exposed image. This technique simply combines the best-exposed portions of each scanned image to make a final image that is closer to what the eye would see. In some cases we made standard color, brightness, and contrast adjustments to further improve quality.

To make the stereo pairs, we overlaid the adjusted left and right images digitally, rotated and nudged them to achieve co-registration, then cropped out the nonoverlapping portions (while maintaining the original 3:2 aspect ratio of a 35 mm slide). Finally, we separated the left and right images and resized the resulting pair to achieve approximately 62 mm of infinity separation, which allows optimal stereo viewing for most people (Ferwerda 1990). We preferred to abut the left and right images without a gutter, which also enables slightly larger stereo images.

The stereo pairs can be viewed with a standard pocket stereoscope, available from forestry supply houses, or with the stereoscope provided. To use the stereoscope provided, hold the stereoscope to your eyes, then hold the stereo pair approximately 8 inches from the stereoscope.

Stereo pictures were not taken at the PP site; there we have only "flat" images.

Hemispherical Photo

We used an off-the-shelf Nikon digital camera fitted with an inexpensive 180 degree fish-eye lens to make an exposure at the center of the plot. The analysis software simply distinguishes light (sky) from dark (biomass). We made these exposures at dawn or dusk when the sky would be evenly lit but the trees would not.

The hemispherical image does not represent what your eye would see standing at the same point; it covers a much wider range. We provide the hemispherical image for comparison with one of your own, if available, and to illustrate the relative changes within a plot at successive stages of sampling. The hemispherical image displayed in each guide page pair was taken at the center of the plot.

The small data table below the hemispherical photo summarizes canopy characteristics measured by analyzing the image with hemiview software:

Gap fraction is the portion of the sky that is not obstructed by canopy. Estimates of gap fraction were obtained on a 25-point grid (5- by 5-m spacing) centered at each plot; the value reported is the average of those 25 readings. Gap fraction at each point was computed for only the top 54 degrees from zenith.

Canopy cover is the inverse of gap fraction (see above), multiplied by 100 to convert to percent basis. It is the average of 25 readings made on a 5 by 5 grid at 5-m spacing.

Canopy Fuel Profile Diagram

We show a diagram of the vertical distribution of available canopy fuel. We smoothed the data by plotting the 3-m running-mean of available canopy bulk density. The relative contribution of branchwood (0 to 3 mm live, 0 to 6 mm dead, plus lichen) is shown by the dashed line. The contribution of foliage is the (horizontal) difference between the total and branchwood lines.

The area "under" the curve (to the left of the lines) is a visual representation of the available canopy fuel load. The actual value for available canopy fuel load is shown on the stand and canopy fuel data table (described below).

To the canopy fuel profile diagrams we annotated our estimates of two important canopy fuel characteristics: canopy base height and canopy bulk density (each quantity is described below).

Stem Diameter Distribution Chart

This chart shows the distribution of trees at each site-stage combination by species and diameter at breast height. We maintained the same X-axis scale among all charts, 0 to 70 cm diameter in 5-cm classes. The Y-axis (trees per hectare) has one of two scales, depending on which site is plotted. The Y-axis for the PP, DFLP, and LP charts goes to 700 trees per hectare, while the SNMC and PPDF charts, with generally larger trees and lower overstory tree density, go only to 200 trees per hectare. The first two stages of the PPDF site exceed this limit in the smallest diameter classes; those bars are truncated, and the actual value for the number of Douglas-fir trees per hectare is annotated.

Stand and Canopy Fuel Data Table

Stand and canopy fuel data is reported by species (if more than one species was present) as well as for the stand as a whole. Details of how each factor was measured or estimated are shown below.

Stem density is the number of live trees per unit plot area greater than or equal to 10 cm diameter.

Basal area is the sum of the outside-bark cross-sectional area at breast height of all live trees per unit plot area.

Branch biomass is the oven-dry mass of live and dead branchwood of all size classes per unit plot area. We obtained this estimate by dividing the sum of live and dead branchwood mass for all trees on the plot by the horizontal plot ground area. Cone biomass is reported here as branch biomass.

Foliage biomass is the oven-dry mass of live and dead foliage per unit plot area. We obtained this estimate by dividing the sum of foliage mass for all trees on the plot by plot area.

Bole biomass is the oven-dry mass of boles (less than 5 cm diameter) of live trees per unit plot area. We obtained this estimate by dividing the sum of bolewood mass for all live trees on the plot by the plot area. To compute bolewood mass for each tree we estimated bole volume by measuring bole diameter at various heights on the bole, then multiplied the volume by species-specific oven-dry bolewood density (Forest Products Laboratory 1999).

Species	Bolewood density kg/m³
Douglas-fir	450
Incense cedar	310[a]
Lodgepole pine	380
Ponderosa pine	380
Subalpine fir	310
White fir	310[b]

[a] The value for western redcedar was used for incense cedar
[b] The value for subalpine fir was used for white fir

Bole biomass is not available for either flaming or smoldering combustion in any type of wildland fire; the values are included here for completeness and for use in estimating potential commercial volume and biomass resulting from alternative treatments.

Biomass of dead standing snags is not included in this guide.

Total aboveground biomass is the oven-dry mass of all living and dead material attached to living trees per unit plot area; here, it is the sum of branch, foliage, and bole biomass.

Canopy fuel load is the oven-dry mass of available canopy fuel per unit ground area. Available canopy fuel is that which is consumed in the short duration flaming front of a crown fire. In this paper it consists of live and dead foliage, 0- to 3-mm live branchwood, 0- to 6-mm dead branchwood, plus any lichen and moss. We estimated canopy fuel load by dividing the sum of available canopy fuel (for all trees in the plot) by the plot area.

Stand height is the average height of the tallest five trees in the plot. Stand height is used in some fire modeling systems to estimate wind reduction factor (the ratio of midflame to open wind speed). Because the sampling stages simulated thinning from below, stand height does not change with sampling stage. At the PPDF and SNMC sites, where fewer than five trees remained in the plot in the final sampling stage, we used the same stand height value as for the preceding stages. Otherwise, using the average height of the remaining trees would have indicated an increase in average stand height at the final sampling stage.

Canopy base height is the lowest height above the ground at which there is sufficient available canopy fuel to propagate fire vertically through the canopy (Scott and Reinhardt 2001). Using a method adapted from Sando and Wick (1972), it is defined here as the lowest height at which at least 0.012 kg per m³ of available canopy fuel was present (Reinhardt and Crookston 2003), using a 3-m-deep running mean to smooth observed values.

Branch height was recorded in 1-m layers, so our estimate of canopy base height has only that level of precision. We assigned canopy base height to the lower boundary of the layer in which the critical level of bulk density occurred. For example, if the critical canopy bulk density occurred in the 4- to 5-m layer, we assigned a canopy base height of 4 m.

Canopy base height is a difficult parameter to measure in the field, and even more difficult to estimate from a tree list or vertical canopy fuel distribution. This study focused on canopy biomass and bulk density rather than canopy base height. Therefore, neither our estimates of canopy base height in this guide nor the method we used to obtain them should be considered final; more research and testing are needed.

Canopy bulk density is the oven-dry mass of available canopy fuel per unit canopy volume (Scott and Reinhardt 2001). Available canopy fuel is defined as the foliage, 0- to 3-mm live branchwood, 0- to 6-mm dead branchwood, and lichen and moss. We estimate ACBD as the maximum 3-m-deep running mean from the CBD profile.

References

Agee, J. K. 1996. The influence of forest structure on fire behavior. In Proceedings of the 17th annual forest vegetation management conference; 1996 January 16-18; Redding, CA 52-68.

Albini, F. A.; Baughman, R. G. 1979. Estimating windspeeds for predicting wildland fire behavior. Res. Pap. INT-221. Ogden, UT U.S. Department of Agriculture, Forest Service, Intermountain Forest and Range Experiment Station. 12 p.

Alexander, M. E. 1988. Help with making crown fire hazard assessments. In Fischer, W. C.; Arno, S. F., comps. Protecting people and homes from wildfire in the Interior West proceedings of the symposium and workshop; 1988 October 6-8; Missoula, MT. Gen. Tech. Rep. INT-251. Ogden, UT U.S. Department of Agriculture, Forest Service, Intermountain Research Station 147-156.

Arno, S. F.; Brown, J. K. 1991. Overcoming the paradox in managing wildland fire. Western Wildlands. 17(1) 40-46.

Asner, G. P.; Scurlock, J. M. O.; Hicke, J. A. 2003. Global synthesis of leaf area index observations implications for ecological and remote sensing studies. Global Ecology and Biogeography. 12 191-205.

Cruz, M. 1999. Modeling the initiation and spread of crown fires. Missoula University of Montana. 157 p. Thesis.

Fahnestock, G. R. 1970. Two keys for appraising forest fuels. Res. Pap. PNW-99. Portland, OR U S. Department of Agriculture, Forest Service, Pacific Northwest Forest and Range Experiment Station. 23 p.

Ferwerda, Jacobus G. 1990. The world of 3-D a practical guide to stereo photography, 2nd ed. Borger, The Netherlands 3-D Book Productions. 300 p.

Finney, M. A. 1998. FARSITE Fire Area Simulator—model development and evaluation. Res. Pap. RMRS-RP-4. Fort Collins, CO U.S. Department of Agriculture, Forest Service, Rocky Mountain Research Station. 47 p.

Forest Products Laboratory. 1999. Wood handbook wood as an engineering material. Gen. Tech. Rep. FPL-GTR-113. Madison, WI U.S. Department of Agriculture, Forest Service, Forest Products Laboratory. 463 p.

Kilgore, B. M.; Sando, R. W. 1975. Crown-fire potential in a sequoia forest after prescribed burning. Forest Science. 21(1) 83-87.

Mutch, R. W.; Arno, S. F.; Brown, J. K.; Carlson, C. E.; Ottmar, R. D.; Peterson, J. L. 1993. Forest health in the Blue Mountains a management strategy for fire-adapted ecosystems. Gen. Tech. Rep. PNW-GTR-310. Portland, OR U.S. Department of Agriculture, Forest Service, Pacific Northwest Research Station. 14 p. (Quigley, T. M., ed.; Forest health in the Blue Mountains science perspectives).

Philpot, C. W.; Mutch, R. W. 1971. The seasonal trend in moisture content, ether extractives, and energy of ponderosa pine and Douglas-fir needles. Res. Pap. INT-112. Ogden, UT U S. Department of Agriculture, Forest Service, Intermountain Forest and Range Experiment Station. 21 p.

Reinhardt, E. D.; Crookston, N. L., tech. eds. 2003. The Fire and fuels extension to the Forest Vegetation Simulator. Gen. Tech. Rep. RMRS-GTR-116. Fort Collins, CO U.S. Department of Agriculture, Forest Service, Rocky Mountain Research Station. 209 p.

Reinhardt, E. D.; Keane, R. E.; Brown, J. K. 1997. First Order Fire Effects Model FOFEM 4.0, user's guide. Gen. Tech. Rep. INT-344. Ogden, UT U.S. Department of Agriculture, Forest Service, Intermountain Research Station. 65 p.

Rothermel, R. C. 1991. Predicting behavior and size of crown fires in the Northern Rocky Mountains. Res. Pap. INT-438. Ogden, UT U.S. Department of Agriculture, Forest Service, Intermountain Research Station. 46 p.

Sando, R. W.; Wick, C. H. 1972. A method of evaluating crown fuels in forest stands. Res. Pap. NC-84. Saint Paul, MN U.S. Department of Agriculture, Forest Service, North Central Forest Experiment Station. 10 p.

Scott, J. H. 1998. Sensitivity analysis of a method for assessing crown fire hazard in the Northern Rocky Mountains, USA. In Viegas, D. X., ed. III international conference on forest fire research; 14th conference on fire and forest meteorology; 1998 November 16-20; Luso, Portugal. Proc. Coimbra, Portugal ADAI. Volume II 2517-2532.

Scott, J. H.; Reinhardt, E. D. 2001. Assessing crown fire potential by linking models of surface and crown fire behavior. Res. Pap. RMRS-RP-29. Fort Collins, CO U.S. Department of Agriculture, Forest Service, Rocky Mountain Research Station. 59 p.

Van Wagner, C. E. 1977. Conditions for the start and spread of crown fire. Canadian Journal of Forest Research. 7 23-34.

Douglas-fir/lodgepole pine
Initial condition

Stereo photo pair

Hemispherical photo

Gap fraction   0.30
Canopy cover (pct)   70

Canopy fuel profile

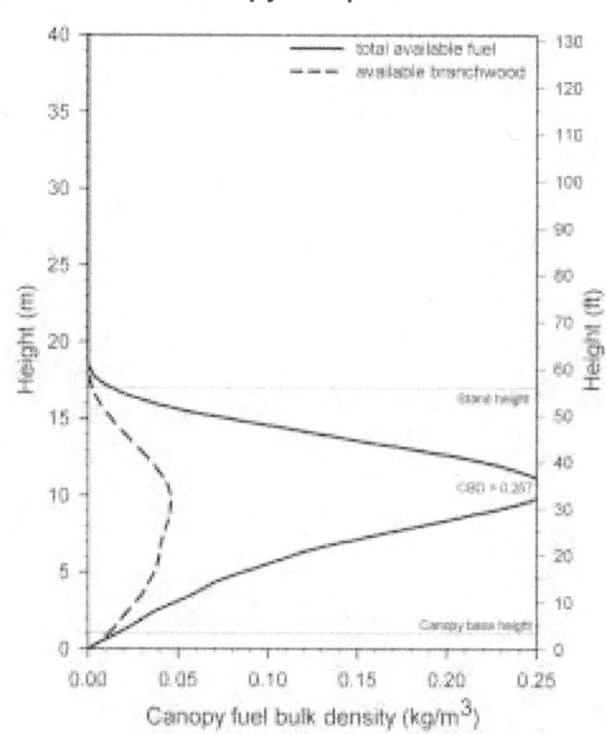

Stem diameter distribution

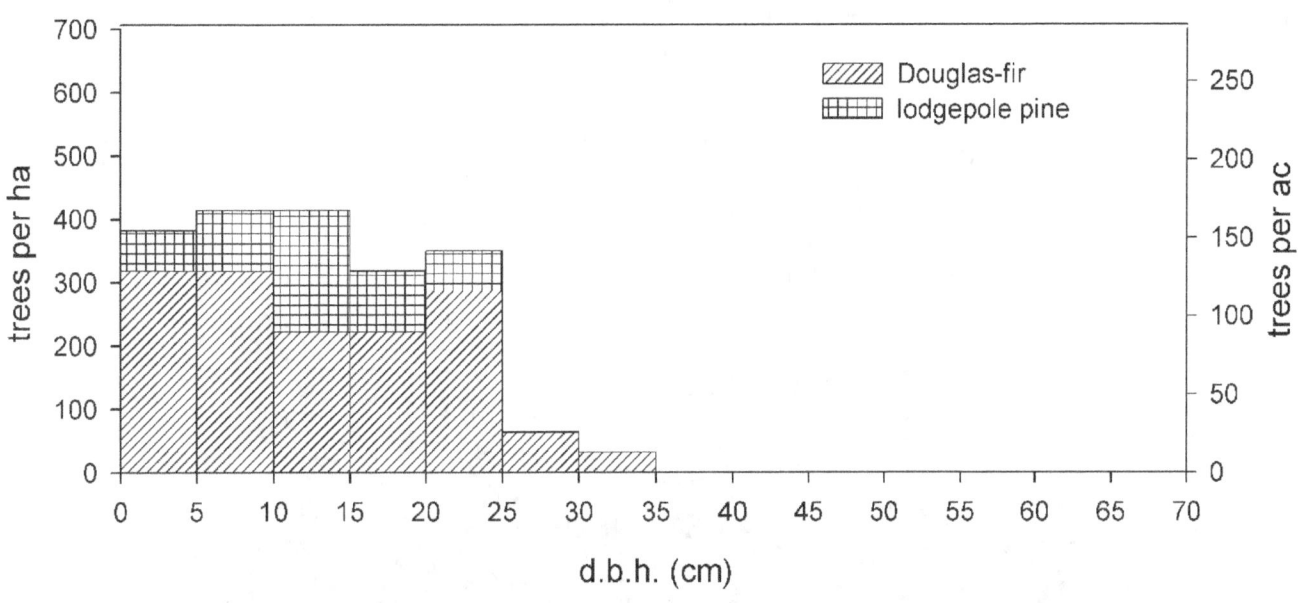

Stand and canopy fuel data

	Units	Douglas-fir	Lodgepole pine	All species
Stem density	trees/ha	828	350	1,178
(≥10 cm)	trees/acre	335	142	477
Basal area	m^2/ha	27.8	8.5	36.3
	ft^2/acre	121	37	158
Branch biomass	kg/m^2	2.59	0.67	3.26
	tons/acre	11.54	2.99	14.53
Foliage biomass	kg/m^2	1.28	0.31	1.59
	tons/acre	5.70	1.39	7.11
Bole biomass	kg/m^2	8.55	2.68	11.22
	tons/acre	38.12	11.95	50.06
Total above-ground biomass	kg/m^2	12.41	3.66	16.07
	tons/acre	55.36	16.33	71.70
Canopy fuel load	kg/m^2	1.69	0.40	2.09
	tons/acre	7.53	1.78	9.31
Stand height	m			17
	ft			56
Canopy base height	m			1
	ft			3
Canopy fuel bulk density	kg/m^3			0.257
	lbs/ft^3			0.0161

Douglas-fir/lodgepole pine
75 percent of initial basal area

Stereo photo pair

Hemispherical photo

Gap fraction   0.41
Canopy cover (pct)   59

Canopy fuel profile

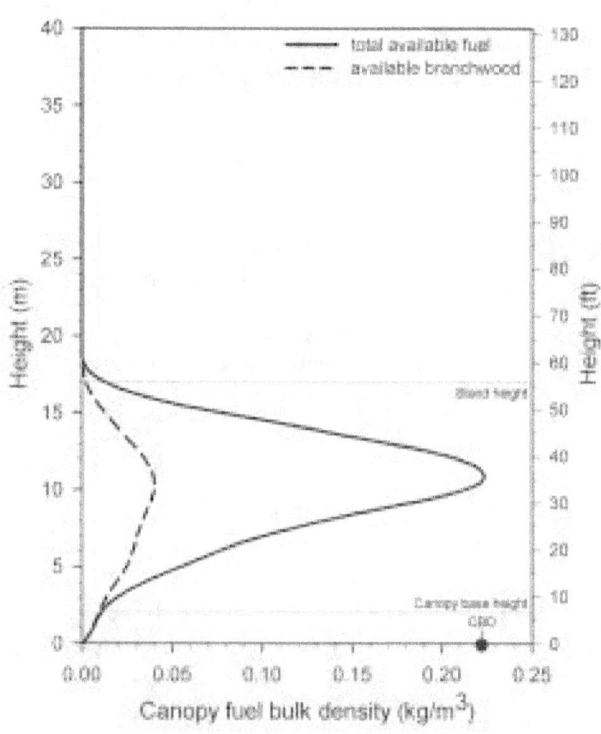

Stem diameter distribution

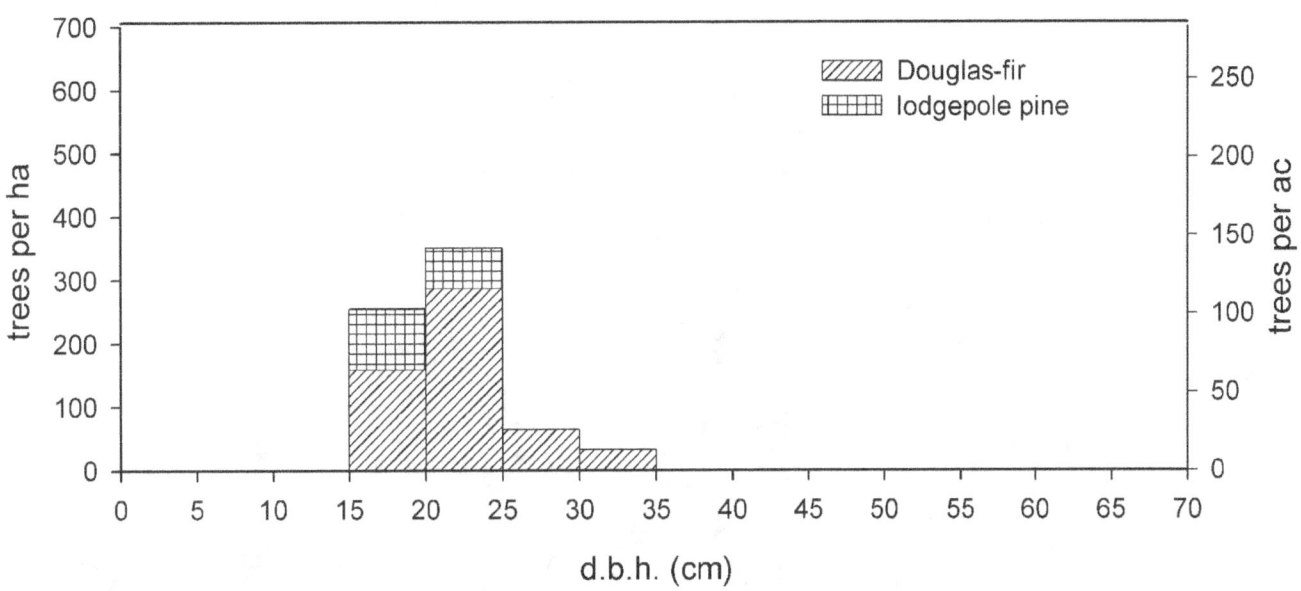

Stand and canopy fuel data

	Units	Douglas-fir	Lodgepole pine	All species
Stem density	trees/ha	541	159	701
(≥10 cm)	trees/acre	219	64	284
Basal area	m^2/ha	22.3	5.0	27.2
	ft^2/acre	97	22	119
Branch biomass	kg/m^2	2.28	0.44	2.71
	tons/acre	10.16	1.95	12.11
Foliage biomass	kg/m^2	1.09	0.20	1.29
	tons/acre	4.87	0.91	5.78
Bole biomass	kg/m^2	7.34	1.49	8.83
	tons/acre	32.74	6.63	39.37
Total above-ground biomass	kg/m^2	10.71	2.13	12.83
	tons/acre	47.77	9.49	57.26
Canopy fuel load	kg/m^2	1.43	0.26	1.69
	tons/acre	6.37	1.15	7.53
Stand height	m			17
	ft			56
Canopy base height	m			2
	ft			7
Canopy fuel bulk density	kg/m^3			0.222
	lbs/ft^3			0.0138

Douglas-fir/lodgepole pine
50 percent of initial basal area

Stereo photo pair

Hemispherical photo

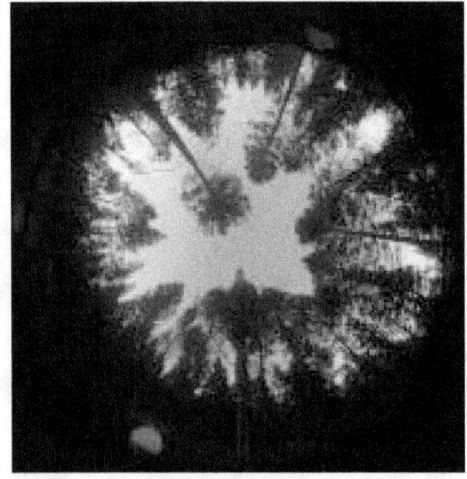

Gap fraction	0.53
Canopy cover (pct)	47

Canopy fuel profile

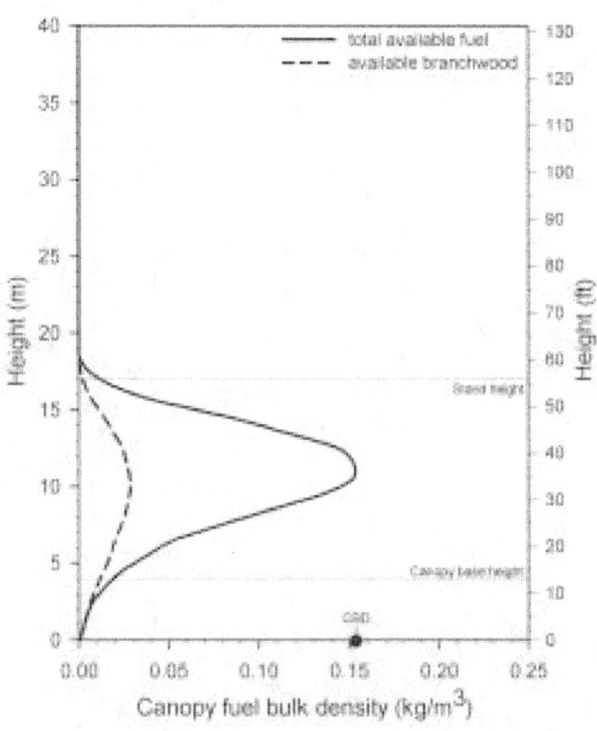

Stem diameter distribution

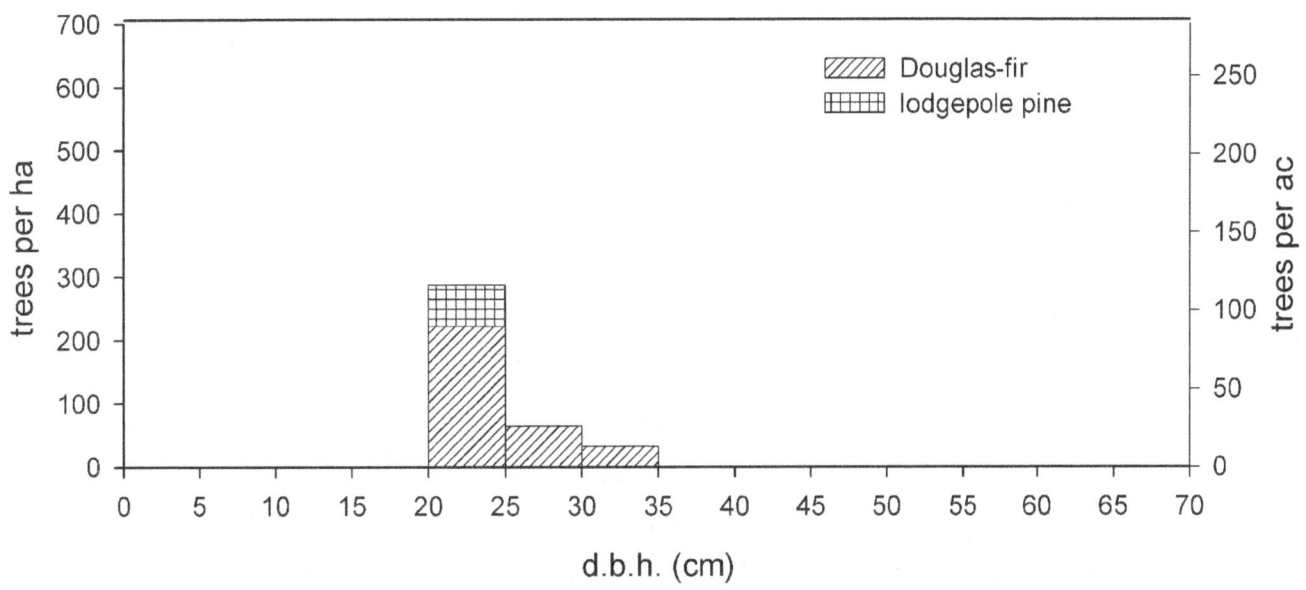

Stand and canopy fuel data

	Units	Douglas-fir	Lodgepole pine	All species
Stem density	trees/ha	318	64	382
(≥10 cm)	trees/acre	129	26	155
Basal area	m²/ha	16.2	2.6	18.8
	ft²/acre	71	11	82
Branch biomass	kg/m²	1.69	0.25	1.94
	tons/acre	7.54	1.12	8.66
Foliage biomass	kg/m²	0.82	0.09	0.90
	tons/acre	3.64	0.39	4.04
Bole biomass	kg/m²	5.51	0.84	6.35
	tons/acre	24.57	3.76	28.33
Total above-	kg/m²	8.02	1.18	9.20
ground biomass	tons/acre	35.76	5.27	41.03
Canopy fuel	kg/m²	1.06	0.13	1.19
load	tons/acre	4.73	0.56	5.29
Stand height	m			17
	ft			56
Canopy base	m			3
height	ft			10
Canopy fuel	kg/m³			0.153
bulk density	lbs/ft³			0.0095

Douglas-fir/lodgepole pine
25 percent of initial basal area

Stereo photo pair

Hemispherical photo

Gap fraction   0.76
Canopy cover (pct)   24

Canopy fuel profile

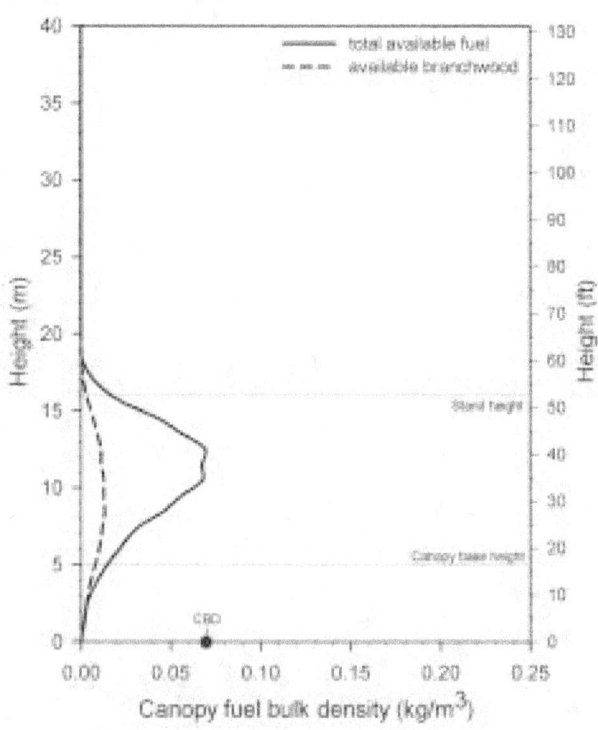

Stem diameter distribution

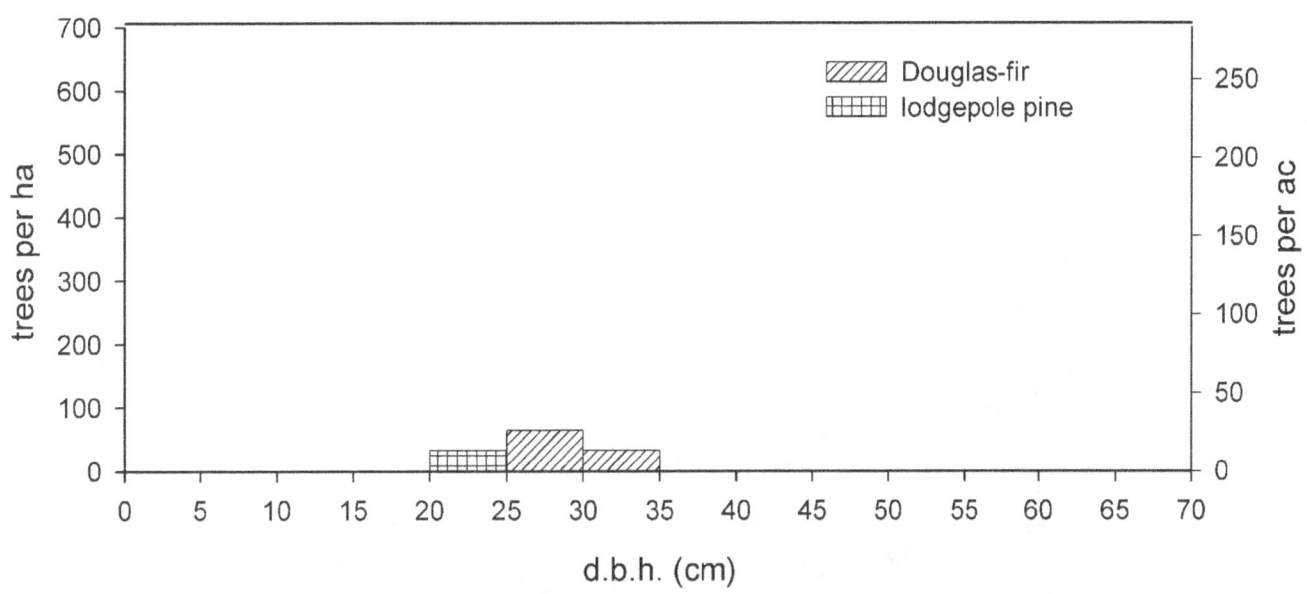

Stand and canopy fuel data

	Units	Douglas-fir	Lodgepole pine	All species
Stem density	trees/ha	96	32	127
(≥10 cm)	trees/acre	39	13	52
Basal area	m²/ha	6.7	1.5	8.2
	ft²/acre	29	6	36
Branch biomass	kg/m²	0.84	0.17	1.01
	tons/acre	3.76	0.74	4.50
Foliage biomass	kg/m²	0.36	0.06	0.41
	tons/acre	1.60	0.25	1.85
Bole biomass	kg/m²	2.54	0.52	3.06
	tons/acre	11.35	2.30	13.66
Total above-ground biomass	kg/m²	3.75	0.74	4.48
	tons/acre	16.71	3.29	20.01
Canopy fuel load	kg/m²	0.47	0.08	0.55
	tons/acre	2.09	0.35	2.45
Stand height	m			16
	ft			52
Canopy base height	m			5
	ft			16
Canopy fuel bulk density	kg/m³			0.069
	lbs/ft³			0.0043

Lodgepole pine
Initial condition

Stereo photo pair

Hemispherical photo

Gap fraction   0.48
Canopy cover (pct)   52

Canopy fuel profile

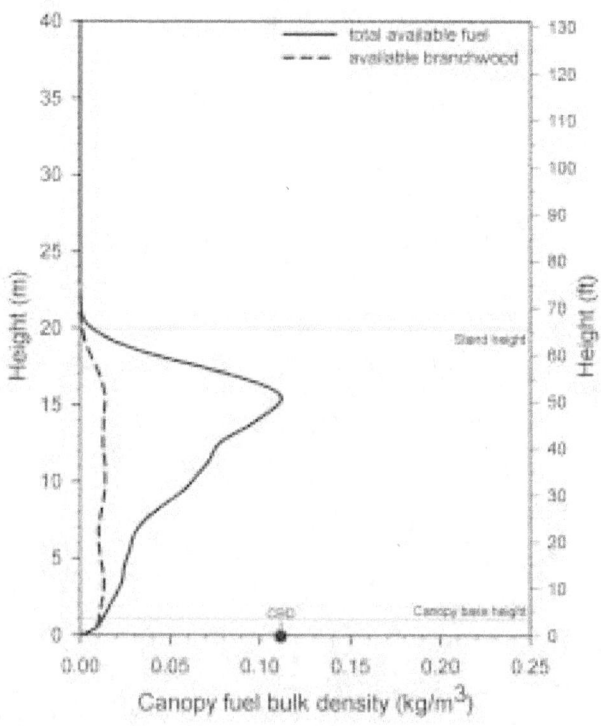

Stem diameter distribution

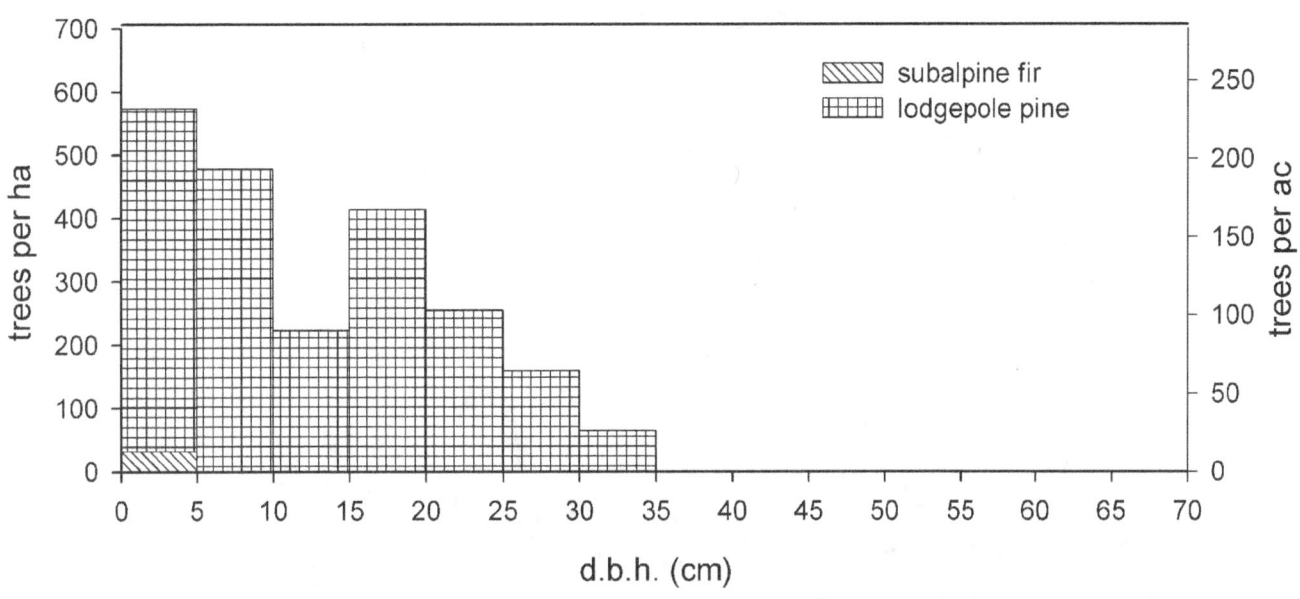

Stand and canopy fuel data

	Units	Subalpine fir	Lodgepole pine	All species
Stem density	trees/ha	0	1,146	1,146
(≥10 cm)	trees/acre	0	464	464
Basal area	m²/ha	0.01	42.7	42.7
	ft²/acre	0.04	186	186
Branch biomass	kg/m²	0.002	2.77	2.77
	tons/acre	0.009	12.34	12.35
Foliage biomass	kg/m²	0.002	0.80	0.80
	tons/acre	0.010	3.57	3.58
Bole biomass	kg/m²	0.002	13.88	13.88
	tons/acre	0.005	61.93	61.93
Total above-ground biomass	kg/m²	0.005	17.45	17.45
	tons/acre	0.023	77.83	77.86
Canopy fuel load	kg/m²	0.003	1.00	1.00
	tons/acre	0.013	4.46	4.47
Stand height	m			20
	ft			66
Canopy base height	m			1
	ft			3
Canopy fuel bulk density	kg/m³			0.112
	lbs/ft³			0.0070

Lodgepole pine
75 percent of initial basal area

Stereo photo pair

Hemispherical photo

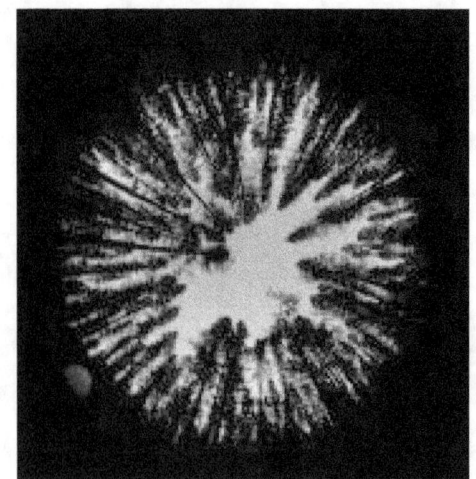

Gap fraction	0.48
Canopy cover (pct)	52

Canopy fuel profile

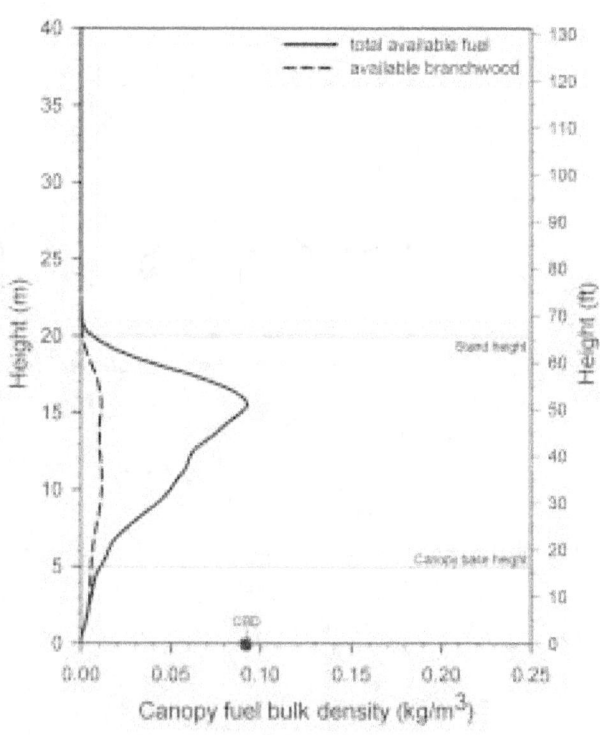

Stem diameter distribution

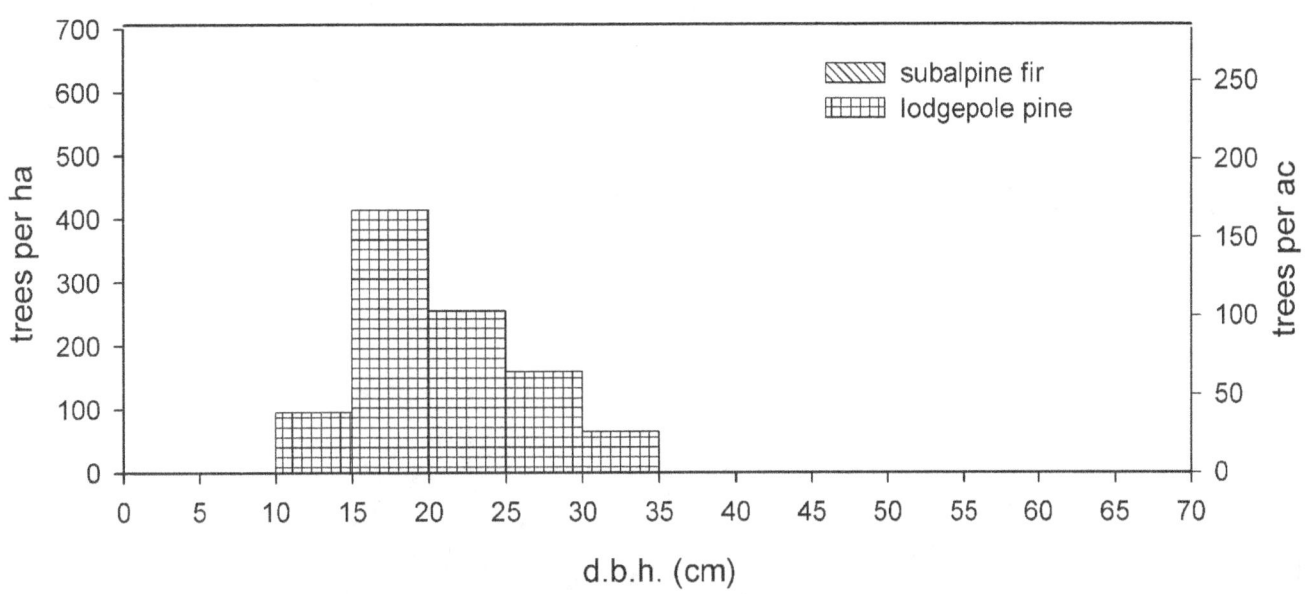

Stand and canopy fuel data

	Units	Subalpine fir	Lodgepole pine	All species
Stem density	trees/ha	0	701	701
(≥10 cm)	trees/acre	0	284	284
Basal area	m²/ha	0.0	32.7	32.7
	ft²/acre	0	142	142
Branch biomass	kg/m²	0.00	2.42	2.42
	tons/acre	0.00	10.78	10.78
Foliage biomass	kg/m²	0.00	0.62	0.62
	tons/acre	0.00	2.77	2.77
Bole biomass	kg/m²	0.00	11.31	11.31
	tons/acre	0.00	50.44	50.44
Total above-ground biomass	kg/m²	0.00	14.34	14.34
	tons/acre	0.00	63.98	63.98
Canopy fuel load	kg/m²	0.00	0.78	0.78
	tons/acre	0.00	3.46	3.46
Stand height	m			20
	ft			66
Canopy base height	m			5
	ft			16
Canopy fuel bulk density	kg/m³			0.093
	lbs/ft³			0.0058

Lodgepole pine
50 percent of initial basal area

Stereo photo pair

Hemispherical photo

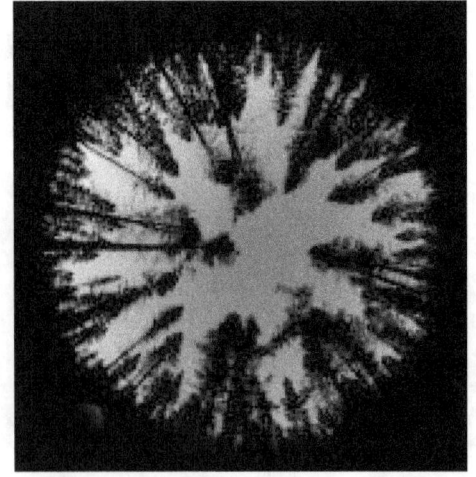

Gap fraction   0.60
Canopy cover (pct)   40

Canopy fuel profile

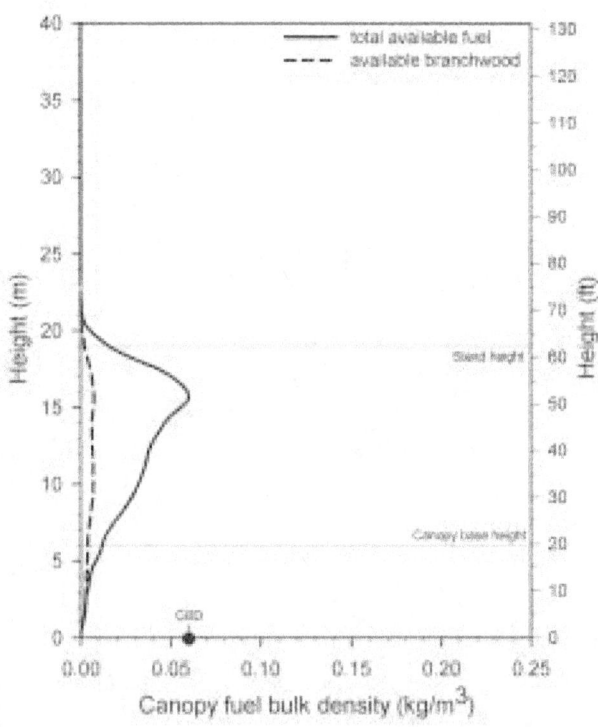

Stem diameter distribution

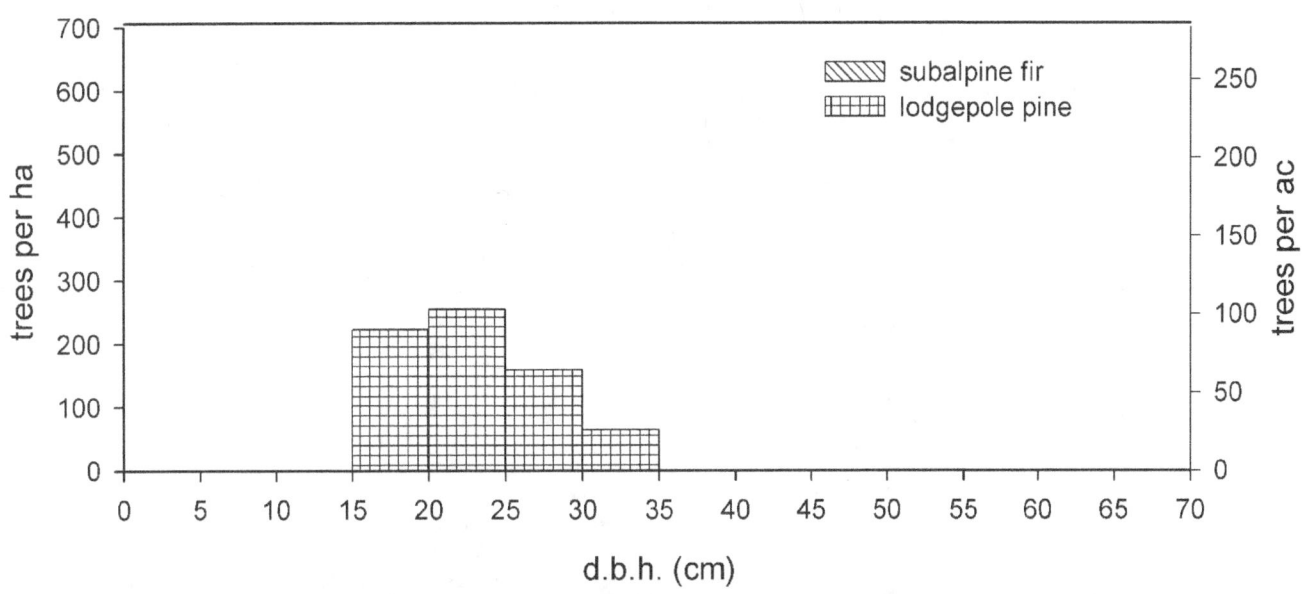

Stand and canopy fuel data

	Units	Subalpine fir	Lodgepole pine	All species
Stem density	trees/ha	0	350	350
(≥10 cm)	trees/acre	0	142	142
Basal area	m²/ha	0.0	21.1	21.1
	ft²/acre	0	92	92
Branch biomass	kg/m²	0.00	1.76	1.76
	tons/acre	0.00	7.87	7.87
Foliage biomass	kg/m²	0.00	0.42	0.42
	tons/acre	0.00	1.86	1.86
Bole biomass	kg/m²	0.00	7.23	7.23
	tons/acre	0.00	32.25	32.25
Total above-	kg/m²	0.00	9.41	9.41
ground biomass	tons/acre	0.00	41.97	41.97
Canopy fuel	kg/m²	0.00	0.51	0.51
load	tons/acre	0.00	2.28	2.28
Stand height	m			19
	ft			62
Canopy base	m			6
height	ft			20
Canopy fuel	kg/m³			0.060
bulk density	lbs/ft³			0.0037

Lodgepole pine
25 percent of initial basal area

Stereo photo pair

Hemispherical photo

Gap fraction   0.76
Canopy cover (pct)   24

Canopy fuel profile

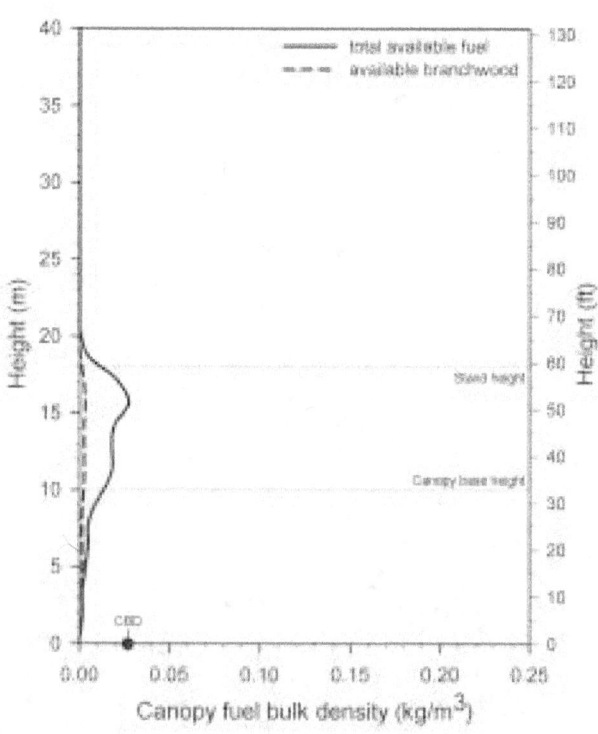

Stem diameter distribution

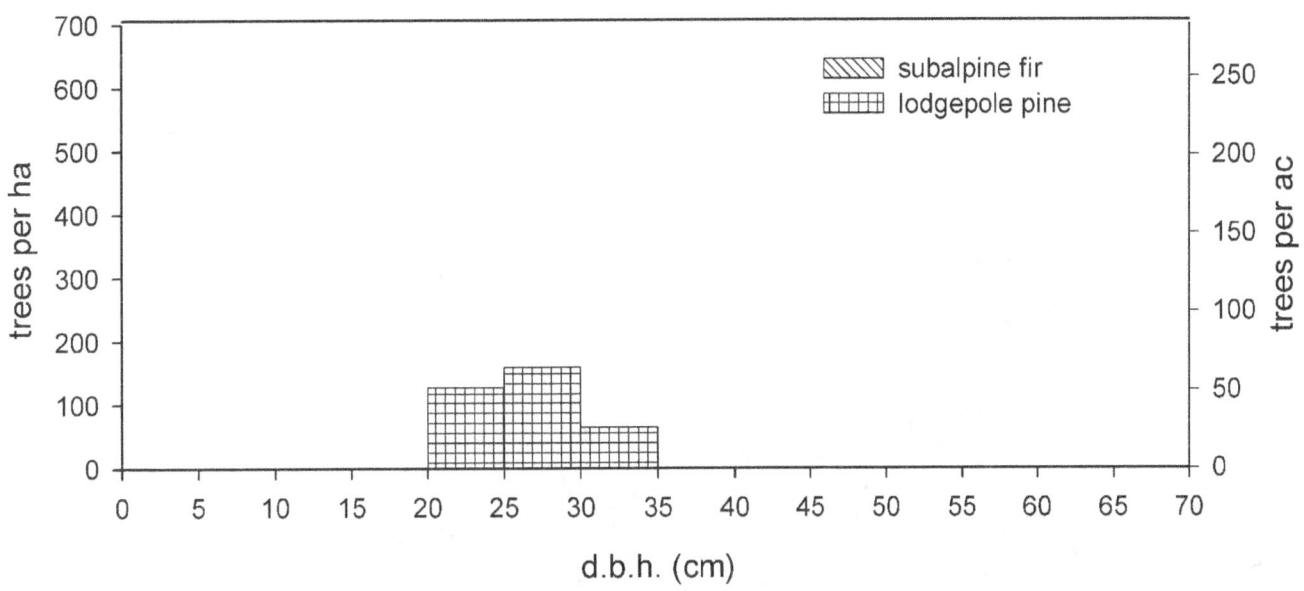

Stand and canopy fuel data

	Units	Subalpine fir	Lodgepole pine	All species
Stem density	trees/ha	0	96	96
(≥10 cm)	trees/acre	0	39	39
Basal area	m²/ha	0.0	7.9	7.9
	ft²/acre	0	34	34
Branch biomass	kg/m²	0.00	0.84	0.84
	tons/acre	0.00	3.75	3.75
Foliage biomass	kg/m²	0.00	0.17	0.17
	tons/acre	0.00	0.77	0.77
Bole biomass	kg/m²	0.00	2.89	2.89
	tons/acre	0.00	12.90	12.90
Total above-ground biomass	kg/m²	0.00	3.91	3.91
	tons/acre	0.00	17.43	17.43
Canopy fuel load	kg/m²	0.00	0.21	0.21
	tons/acre	0.00	0.94	0.94
Stand height	m			18
	ft			59
Canopy base height	m			10
	ft			33
Canopy fuel bulk density	kg/m³			0.028
	lbs/ft³			0.0017

Ponderosa pine/Douglas-fir
Initial condition

Stereo photo pair

Hemispherical photo

Gap fraction	0.41
Canopy cover (pct)	59

Canopy fuel profile

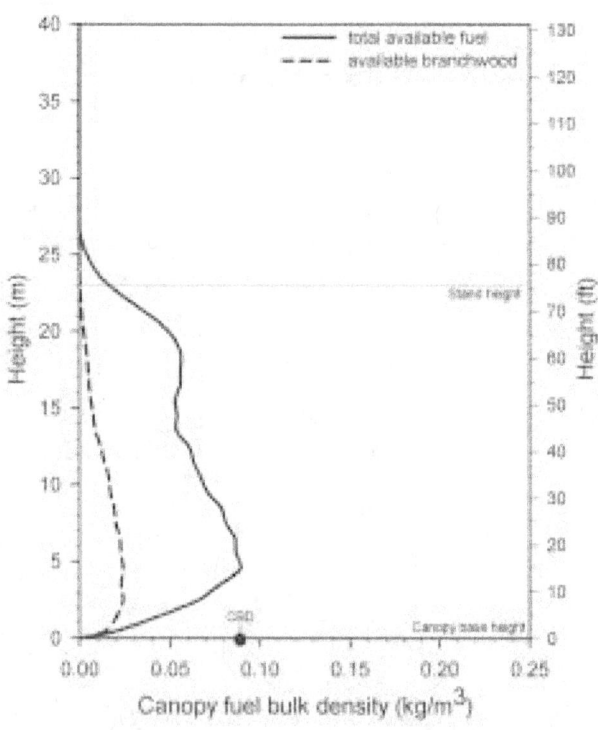

Stem diameter distribution

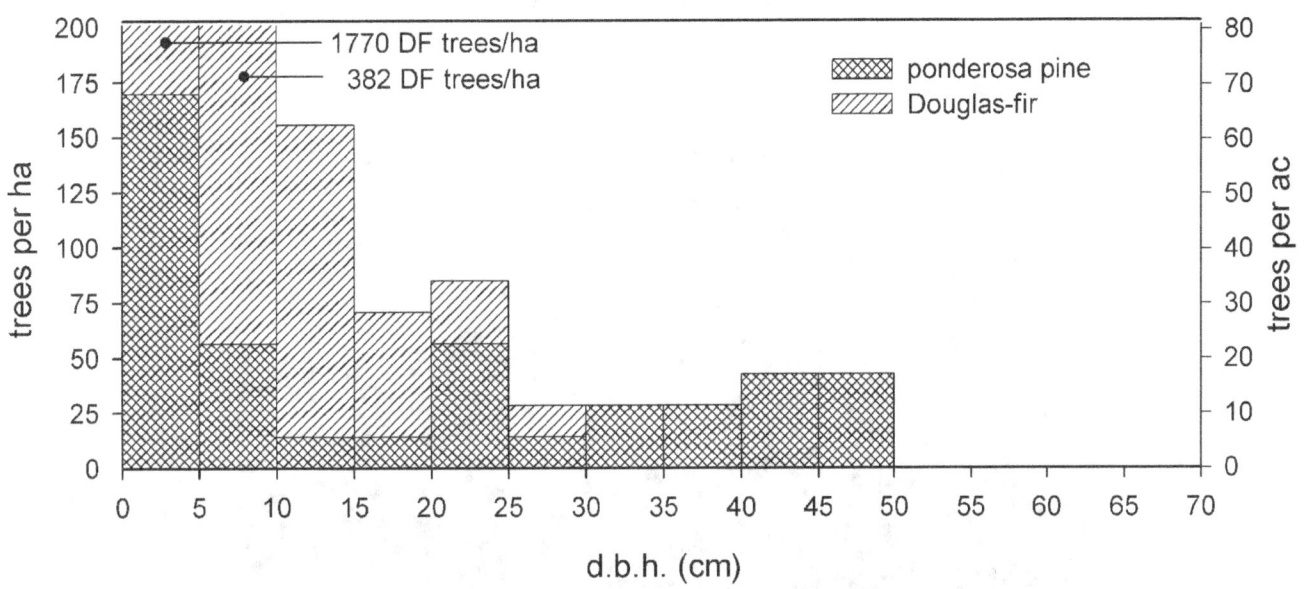

Stand and canopy fuel data

	Units	Douglas-fir	Ponderosa pine	All species
Stem density	trees/ha	241	241	481
(≥10 cm)	trees/acre	97	97	195
Basal area	m²/ha	7.8	22.6	30.4
	ft²/acre	34	99	133
Branch biomass	kg/m²	1.01	2.17	3.18
	tons/acre	4.51	9.67	14.18
Foliage biomass	kg/m²	0.65	0.46	1.11
	tons/acre	2.89	2.05	4.93
Bole biomass	kg/m²	1.90	8.18	10.08
	tons/acre	8.46	36.49	44.95
Total above-ground biomass	kg/m²	3.56	10.81	14.36
	tons/acre	15.86	48.20	64.06
Canopy fuel load	kg/m²	0.89	0.51	1.40
	tons/acre	3.99	2.27	6.26
Stand height	m			23
	ft			75
Canopy base height	m			0
	ft			0
Canopy fuel bulk density	kg/m³			0.089
	lbs/ft³			0.0056

Ponderosa pine/Douglas-fir
Understory removed (≤5 cm)

Stereo photo pair

Hemispherical photo

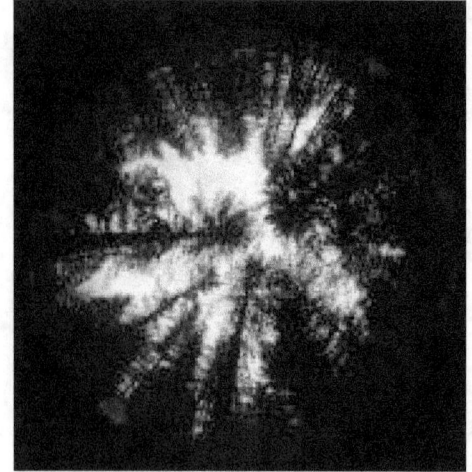

Gap fraction   0.41
Canopy cover (pct)   59

Canopy fuel profile

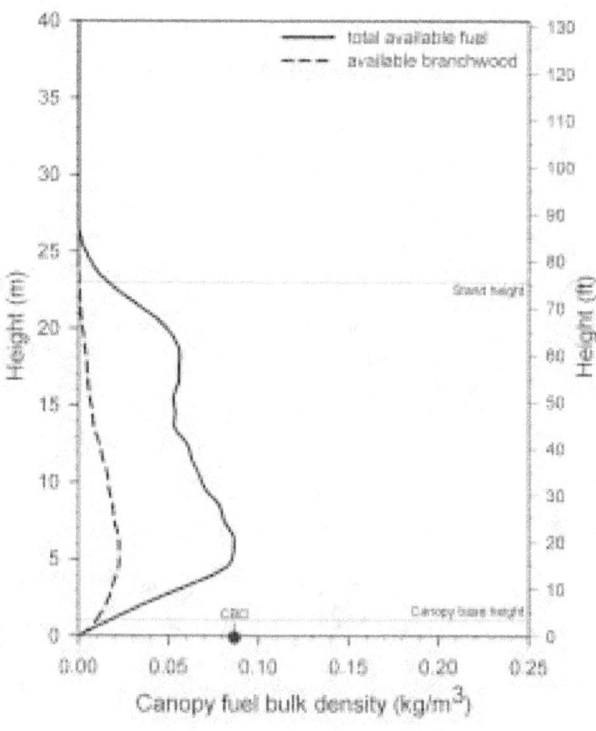

Stem diameter distribution

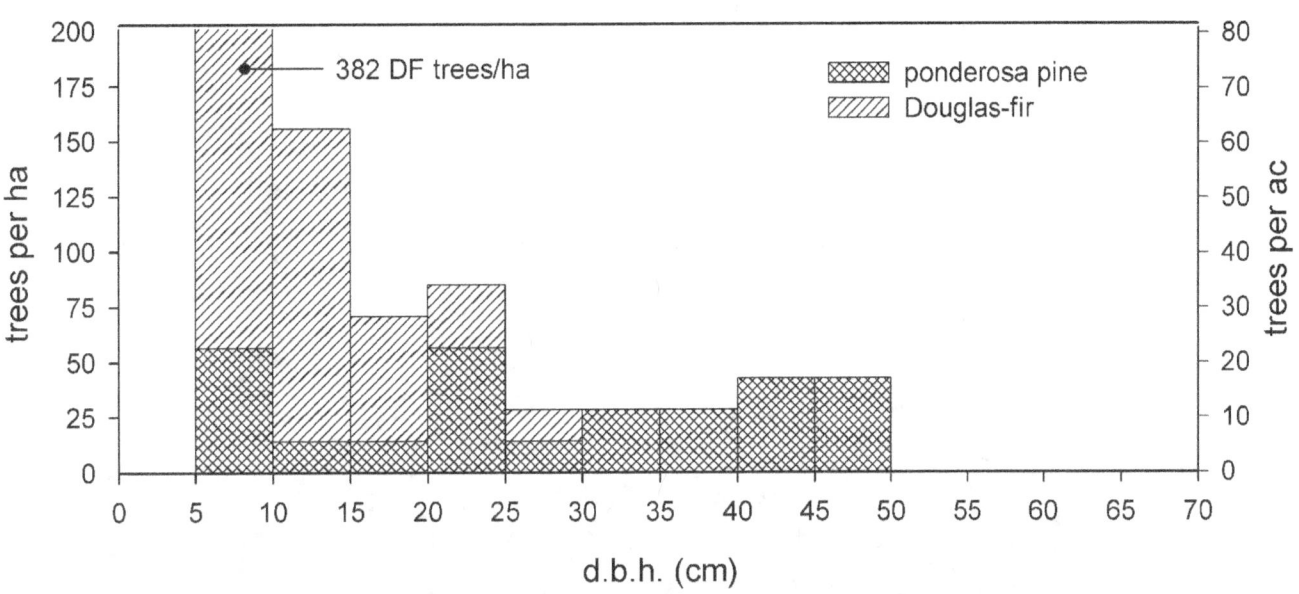

Stand and canopy fuel data

	Units	Douglas-fir	Ponderosa pine	All species
Stem density	trees/ha	241	241	481
(≥10 cm)	trees/acre	97	97	195
Basal area	m²/ha	7.3	22.5	30.0
	ft²/acre	32	98	129
Branch biomass	kg/m²	0.95	2.17	3.11
	tons/acre	4.23	9.63	13.86
Foliage biomass	kg/m²	0.60	0.46	1.06
	tons/acre	2.67	2.04	4.72
Bole biomass	kg/m²	1.84	8.14	9.98
	tons/acre	8.19	36.33	44.52
Total above-	kg/m²	3.38	10.76	14.14
ground biomass	tons/acre	15.10	48.00	63.10
Canopy fuel	kg/m²	0.82	0.51	1.33
load	tons/acre	3.66	2.26	5.92
Stand height	m			23
	ft			75
Canopy base	m			1
height	ft			3
Canopy fuel	kg/m³			0.086
bulk density	lbs/ft³			0.0054

Ponderosa pine/Douglas-fir
75 percent of initial basal area

Stereo photo pair

Hemispherical photo

Gap fraction   0.50
Canopy cover (pct)   50

Canopy fuel profile

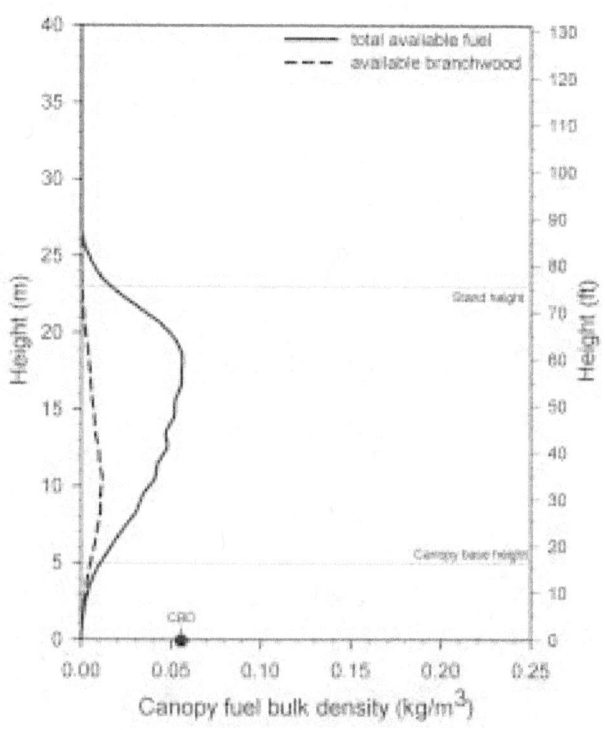

Stem diameter distribution

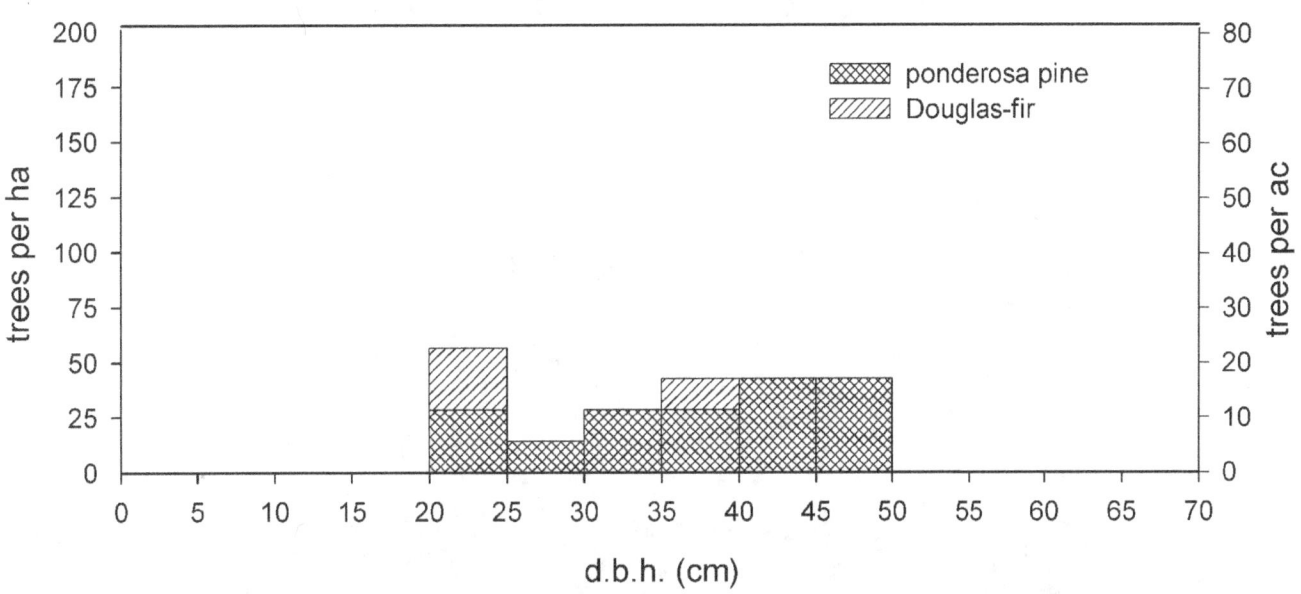

Stand and canopy fuel data

	Units	Douglas-fir	Ponderosa pine	All species
Stem density	trees/ha	42	184	226
(≥10 cm)	trees/acre	17	74	92
Basal area	m²/ha	2.6	20.8	23.3
	ft²/acre	11	90	102
Branch biomass	kg/m²	0.44	2.07	2.50
	tons/acre	1.96	9.21	11.17
Foliage biomass	kg/m²	0.20	0.44	0.63
	tons/acre	0.88	1.95	2.83
Bole biomass	kg/m²	0.86	7.80	8.65
	tons/acre	3.82	34.78	38.60
Total above-ground biomass	kg/m²	1.49	10.30	11.79
	tons/acre	6.66	45.93	52.59
Canopy fuel load	kg/m²	0.28	0.48	0.76
	tons/acre	1.27	2.14	3.41
Stand height	m			23
	ft			75
Canopy base height	m			5
	ft			16
Canopy fuel bulk density	kg/m³			0.055
	lbs/ft³			0.0034

Ponderosa pine/Douglas-fir
50 percent of initial basal area

Stereo photo pair

Hemispherical photo

Gap fraction   0.70
Canopy cover (pct)   30

Canopy fuel profile

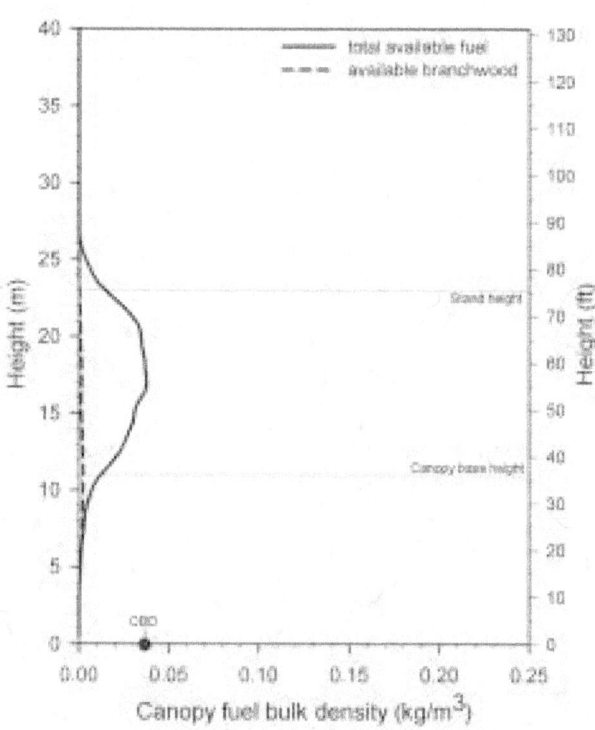

Stem diameter distribution

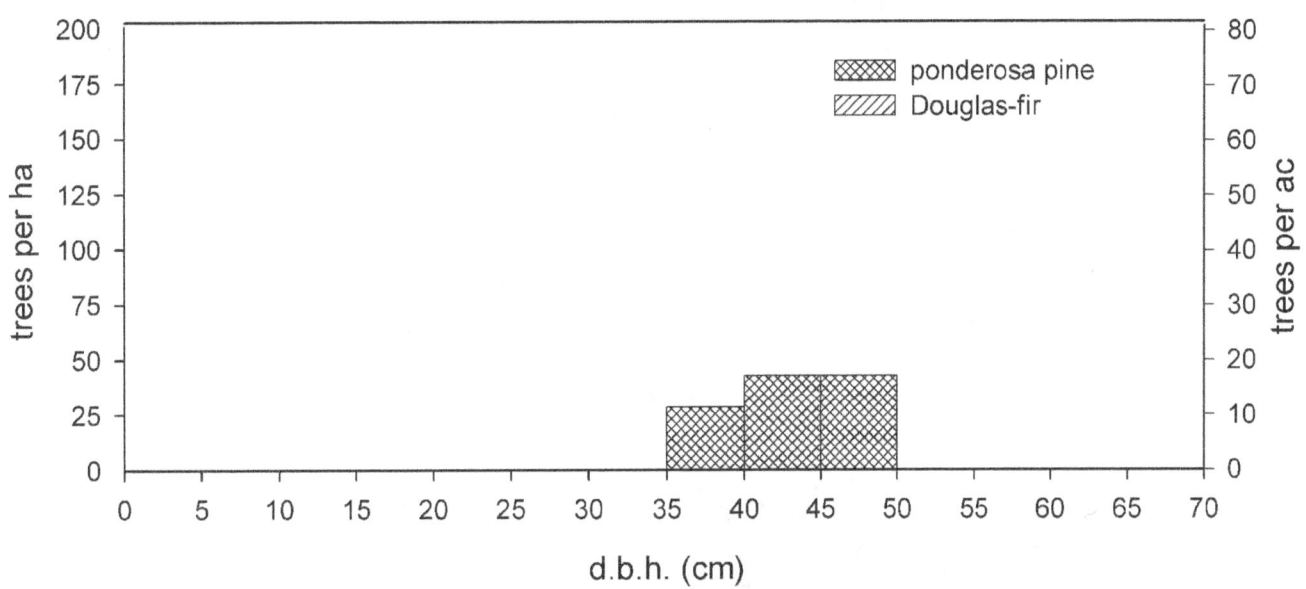

Stand and canopy fuel data

	Units	Douglas-fir	Ponderosa pine	All species
Stem density	trees/ha	0	113	113
(≥10 cm)	trees/acre	0	46	46
Basal area	m²/ha	0.0	16.6	16.6
	ft²/acre	0	72	72
Branch biomass	kg/m²	0.00	1.76	1.76
	tons/acre	0.00	7.85	7.85
Foliage biomass	kg/m²	0.00	0.37	0.37
	tons/acre	0.00	1.65	1.65
Bole biomass	kg/m²	0.00	6.32	6.32
	tons/acre	0.00	28.21	28.21
Total above-ground biomass	kg/m²	0.00	8.45	8.45
	tons/acre	0.00	37.70	37.70
Canopy fuel load	kg/m²	0.00	0.40	0.40
	tons/acre	0.00	1.79	1.79
Stand height	m			23
	ft			75
Canopy base height	m			11
	ft			36
Canopy fuel bulk density	kg/m³			0.037
	lbs/ft³			0.0023

Ponderosa pine/Douglas-fir
25 percent of initial basal area

Stereo photo

Stereo
photo
not
available

Hemispherical photo

Gap fraction   0.81
Canopy cover (pct)   19

Canopy fuel profile

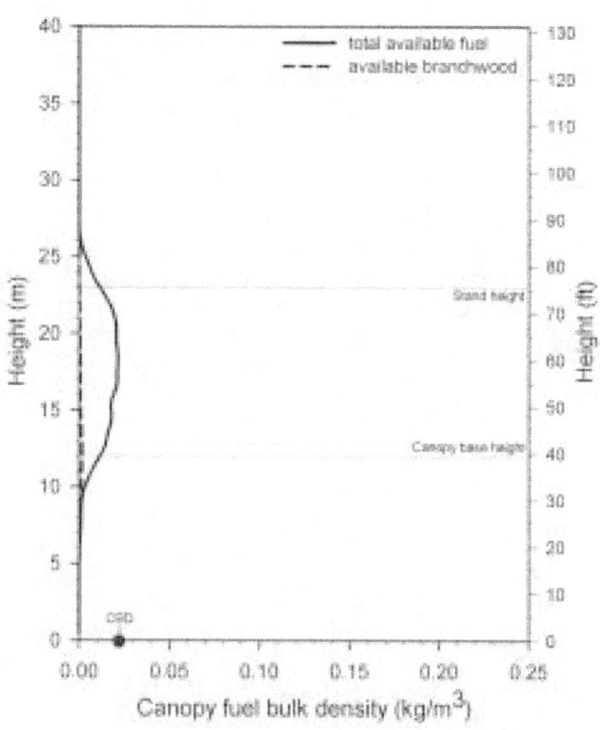

Stem diameter distribution

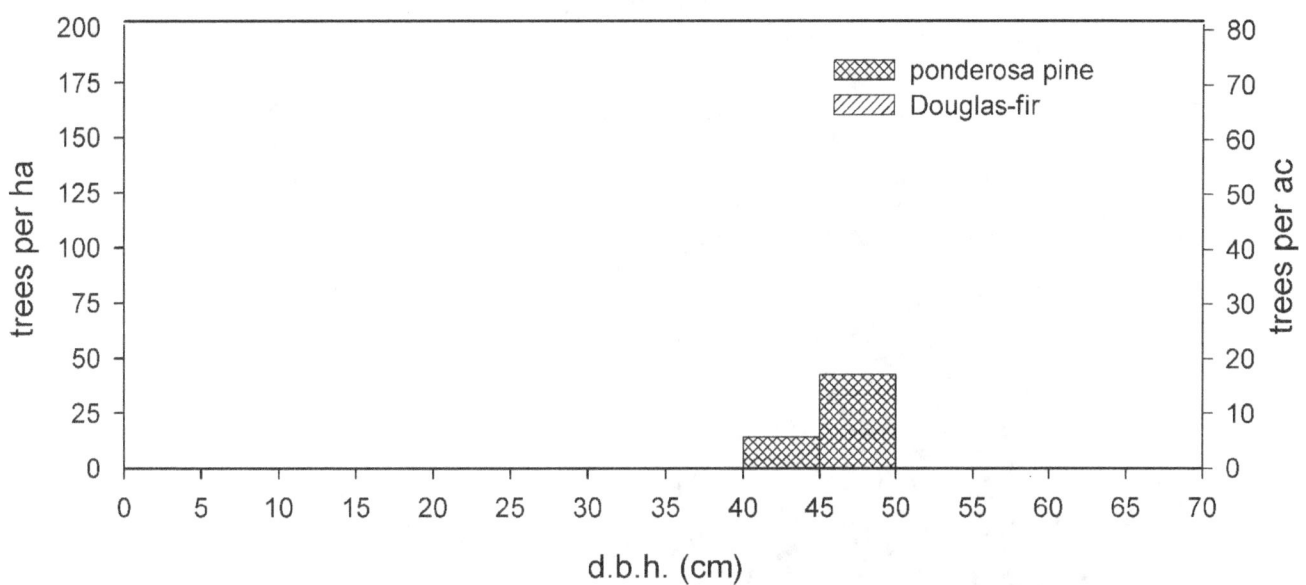

Stand and canopy fuel data

	Units	Douglas-fir	Ponderosa pine	All species
Stem density	trees/ha	0	57	57
(≥10 cm)	trees/acre	0	23	23
Basal area	m²/ha	0.0	9.2	9.2
	ft²/acre	0	40	40
Branch biomass	kg/m²	0.00	0.99	0.99
	tons/acre	0.00	4.42	4.42
Foliage biomass	kg/m²	0.00	0.22	0.22
	tons/acre	0.00	1.00	1.00
Bole biomass	kg/m²	0.00	3.44	3.44
	tons/acre	0.00	15.36	15.36
Total above-ground biomass	kg/m²	0.00	4.66	4.66
	tons/acre	0.00	20.78	20.78
Canopy fuel load	kg/m²	0.00	0.24	0.24
	tons/acre	0.00	1.05	1.05
Stand height	m			23
	ft			75
Canopy base height	m			12
	ft			39
Canopy fuel bulk density	kg/m³			0.022
	lbs/ft³			0.0014

Ponderosa pine
Initial condition

Stereo photo

Stereo
photo
not
available

Hemispherical photo

Gap fraction	0.31
Canopy cover (pct)	69

Canopy fuel profile

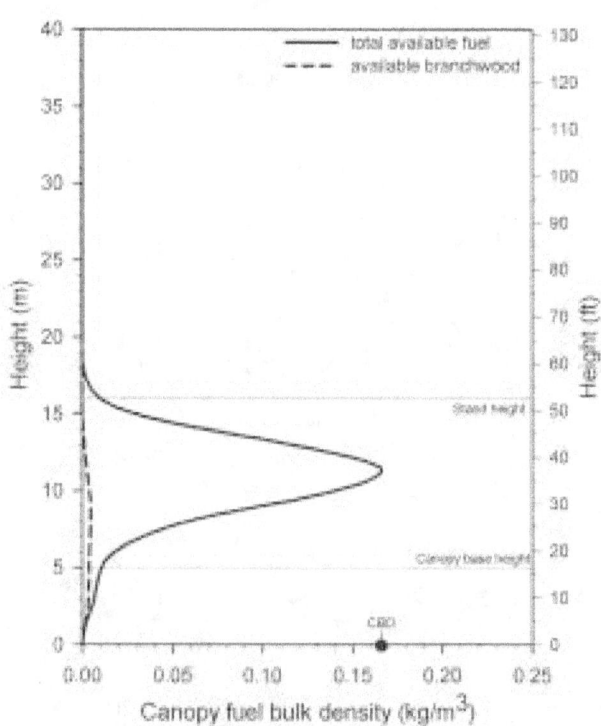

Stem diameter distribution

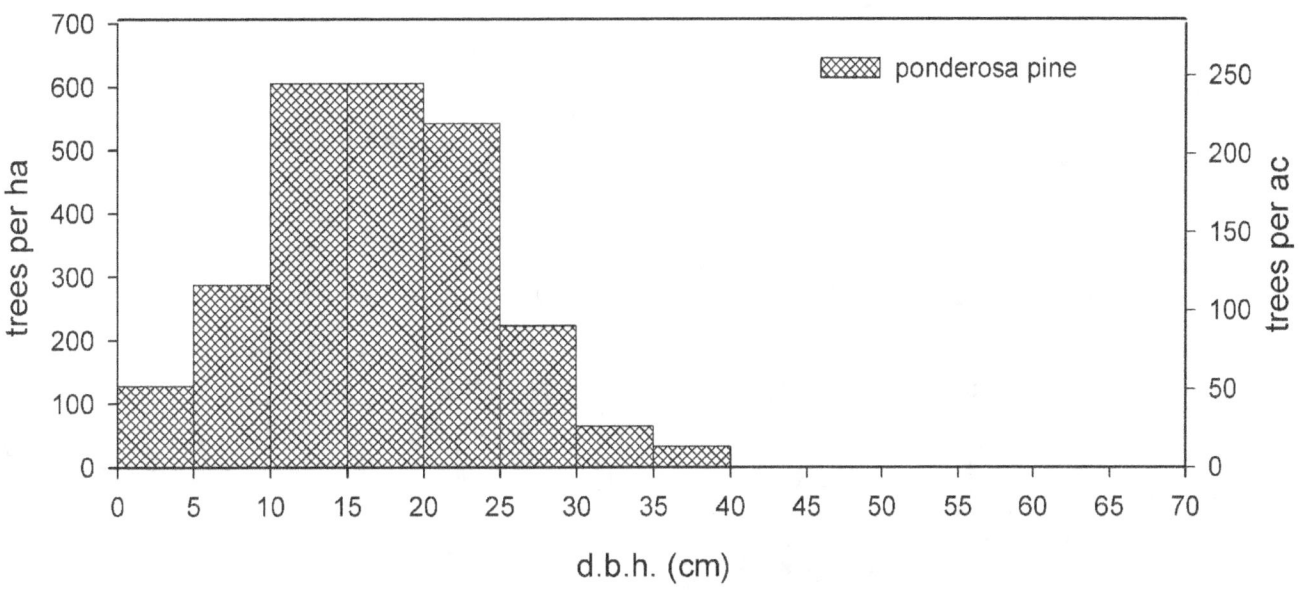

Stand and canopy fuel data

	Units	Ponderosa pine
Stem density (≥10 cm)	trees/ha	2,070
	trees/acre	838
Basal area	m^2/ha	69.0
	ft^2/acre	301
Branch biomass	kg/m^2	3.66
	tons/acre	16.32
Foliage biomass	kg/m^2	0.88
	tons/acre	3.94
Bole biomass	kg/m^2	16.53
	tons/acre	73.73
Total above-ground biomass	kg/m^2	21.07
	tons/acre	93.99
Canopy fuel load	kg/m^2	0.93
	tons/acre	4.14
Stand height	m	16
	ft	52
Canopy base height	m	5
	ft	16
Canopy fuel bulk density	kg/m^3	0.166
	lbs/ft^3	0.0104

Ponderosa pine
75 percent of initial basal area

Stereo photo

Stereo
photo
not
available

Hemispherical photo

Gap fraction   0.48
Canopy cover (pct)   52

Canopy fuel profile

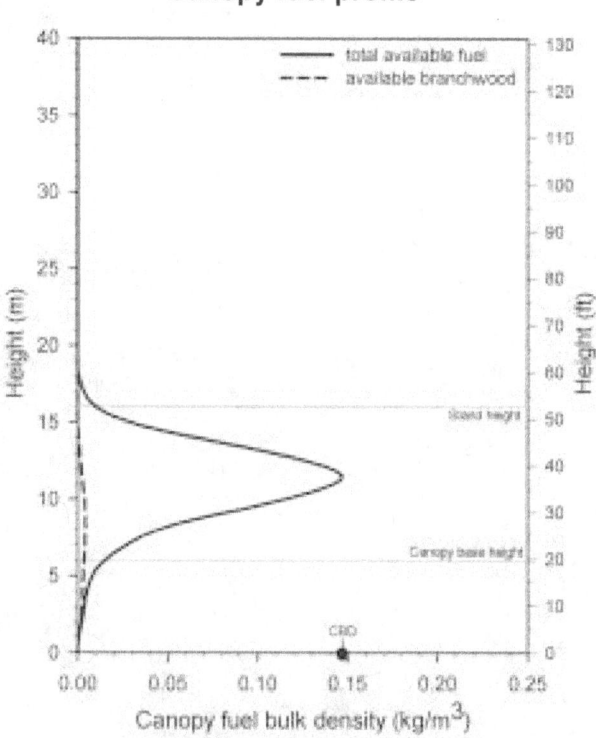

Stem diameter distribution

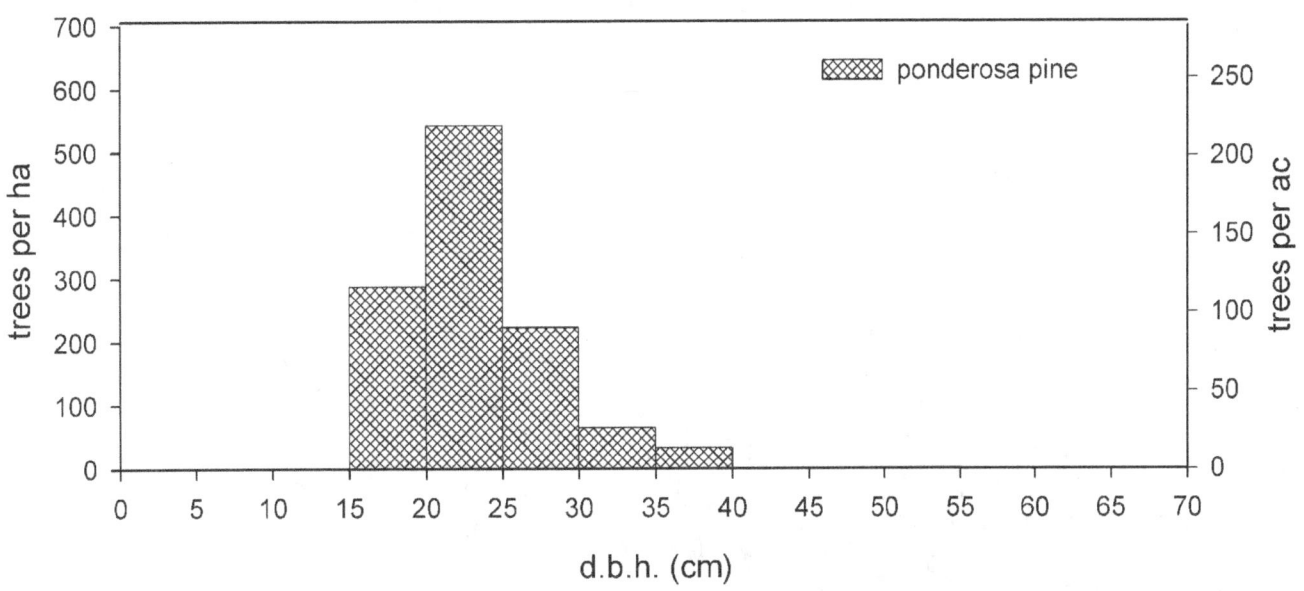

Stand and canopy fuel data

	Units	Ponderosa pine
Stem density (≥10 cm)	trees/ha	1,146
	trees/acre	464
Basal area	m^2/ha	53.2
	ft^2/acre	232
Branch biomass	kg/m^2	3.34
	tons/acre	14.92
Foliage biomass	kg/m^2	0.76
	tons/acre	3.39
Bole biomass	kg/m^2	13.11
	tons/acre	58.49
Total above-ground biomass	kg/m^2	17.22
	tons/acre	76.80
Canopy fuel load	kg/m^2	0.80
	tons/acre	3.56
Stand height	m	16
	ft	52
Canopy base height	m	6
	ft	20
Canopy fuel bulk density	kg/m^3	0.147
	lbs/ft^3	0.0092

Ponderosa pine
50 percent of initial basal area

Stereo photo

Stereo
photo
not
available

Hemispherical photo

Gap fraction   0.53
Canopy cover (pct)   47

Canopy fuel profile

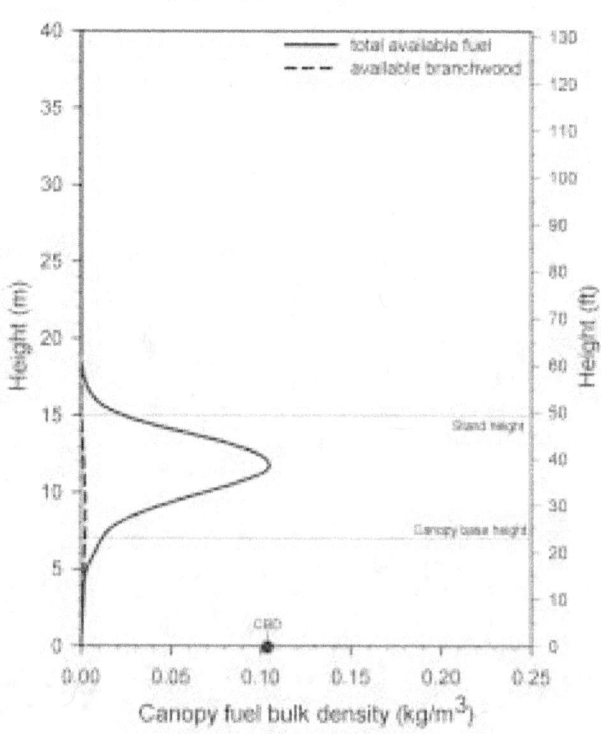

Stem diameter distribution

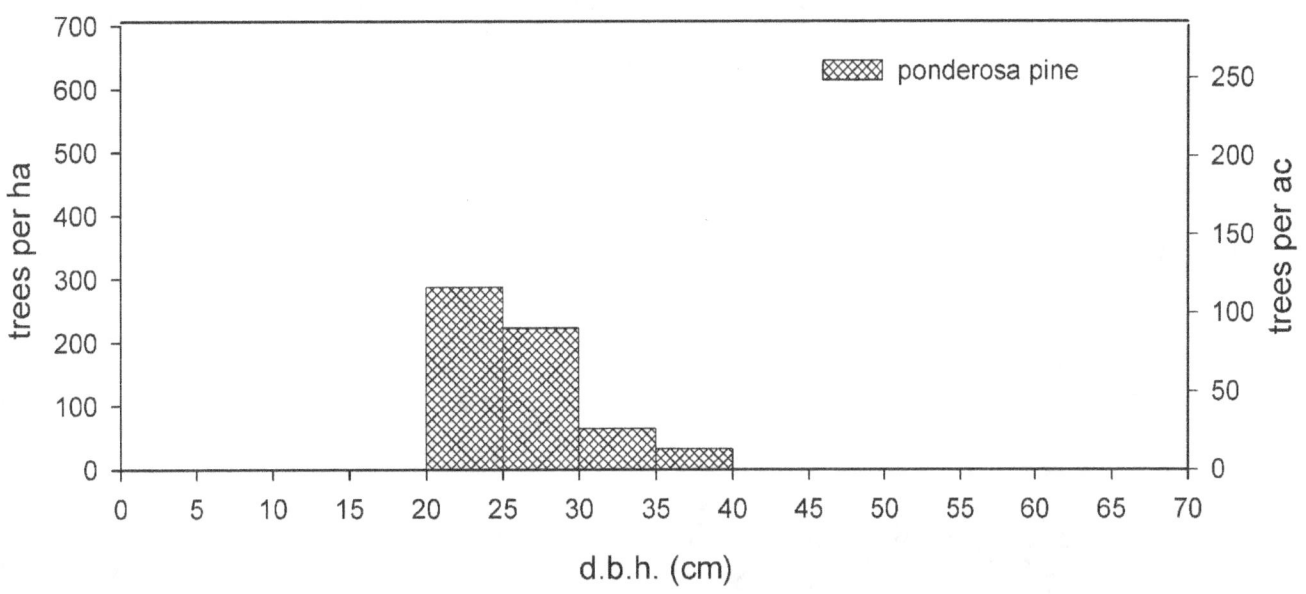

Stand and canopy fuel data

	Units	Ponderosa pine
Stem density	trees/ha	605
(≥10 cm)	trees/acre	245
Basal area	m^2/ha	35.9
	ft^2/acre	156
Branch biomass	kg/m^2	2.43
	tons/acre	10.83
Foliage biomass	kg/m^2	0.51
	tons/acre	2.28
Bole biomass	kg/m^2	9.06
	tons/acre	40.44
Total above-	kg/m^2	12.00
ground biomass	tons/acre	53.54
Canopy fuel	kg/m^2	0.53
load	tons/acre	2.38
Stand height	m	15
	ft	49
Canopy base	m	7
height	ft	23
Canopy fuel	kg/m^3	0.104
bulk density	lbs/ft^3	0.0065

Ponderosa pine
25 percent of initial basal area

Stereo photo

Stereo
photo
not
available

Hemispherical photo

Gap fraction   0.77
Canopy cover (pct)   23

Canopy fuel profile

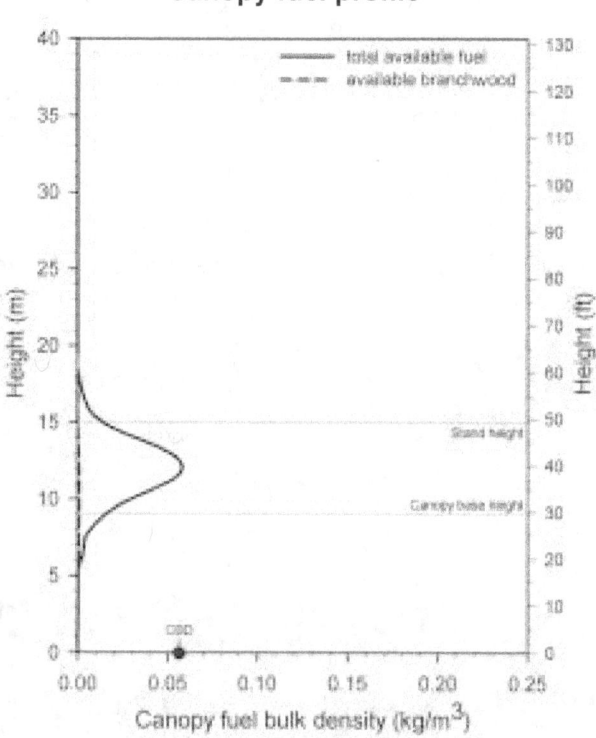

Stem diameter distribution

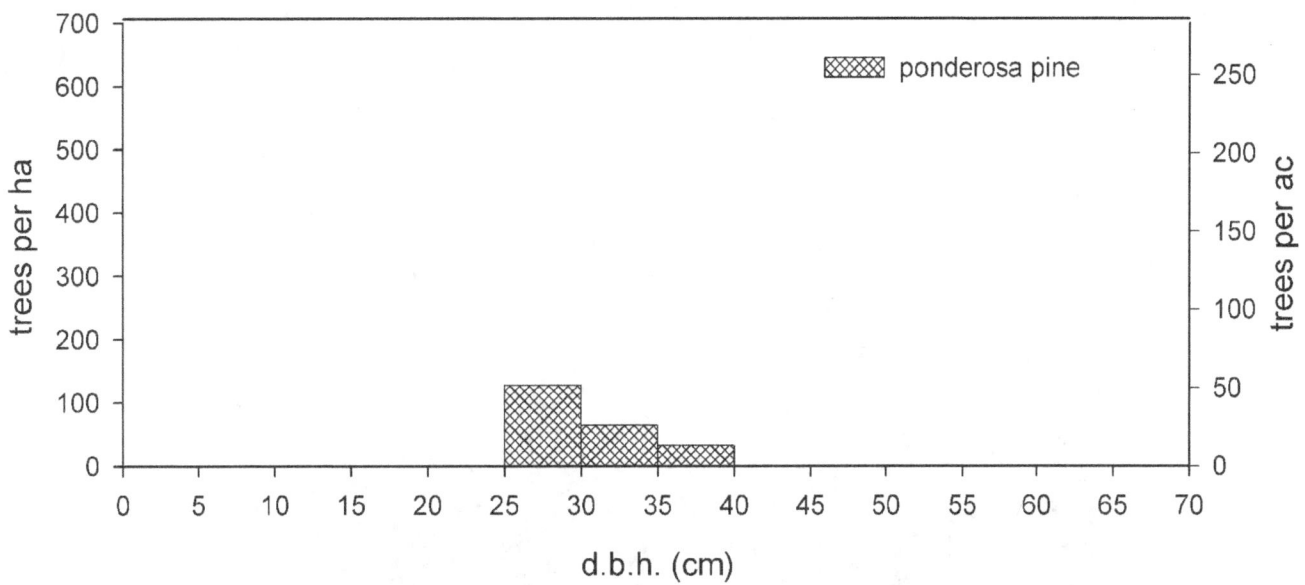

Stand and canopy fuel data

	Units	Ponderosa pine
Stem density (≥10 cm)	trees/ha	223
	trees/acre	90
Basal area	m²/ha	17.8
	ft²/acre	77
Branch biomass	kg/m²	1.28
	tons/acre	5.69
Foliage biomass	kg/m²	0.26
	tons/acre	1.17
Bole biomass	kg/m²	4.57
	tons/acre	20.40
Total above-ground biomass	kg/m²	6.11
	tons/acre	27.27
Canopy fuel load	kg/m²	0.27
	tons/acre	1.21
Stand height	m	15
	ft	49
Canopy base height	m	9
	ft	30
Canopy fuel bulk density	kg/m³	0.057
	lbs/ft³	0.0036

Sierra Nevada mixed conifer
Initial condition

Stereo photo pair

Hemispherical photo

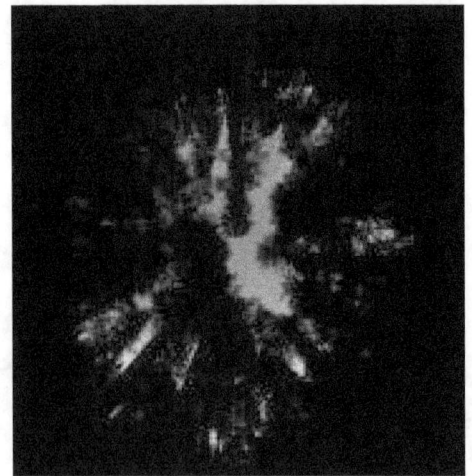

| Gap fraction | 0.26 |
| Canopy cover (pct) | 74 |

Canopy fuel profile

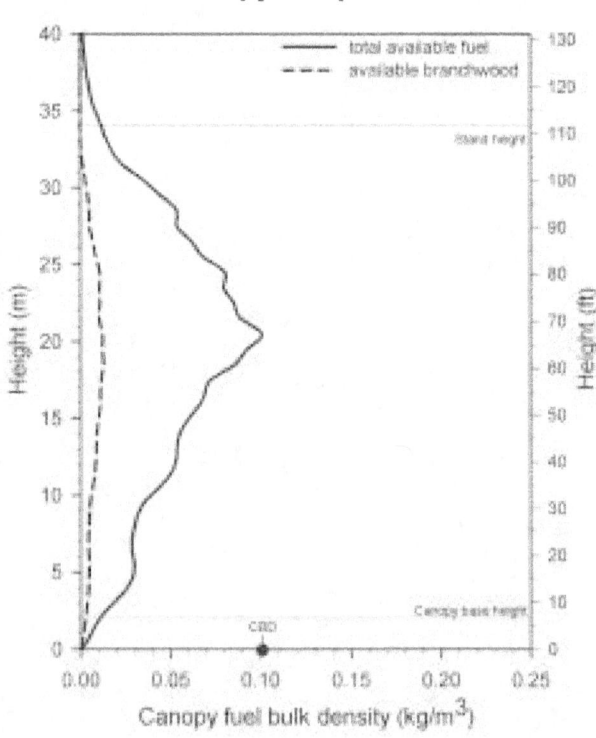

Stem diameter distribution

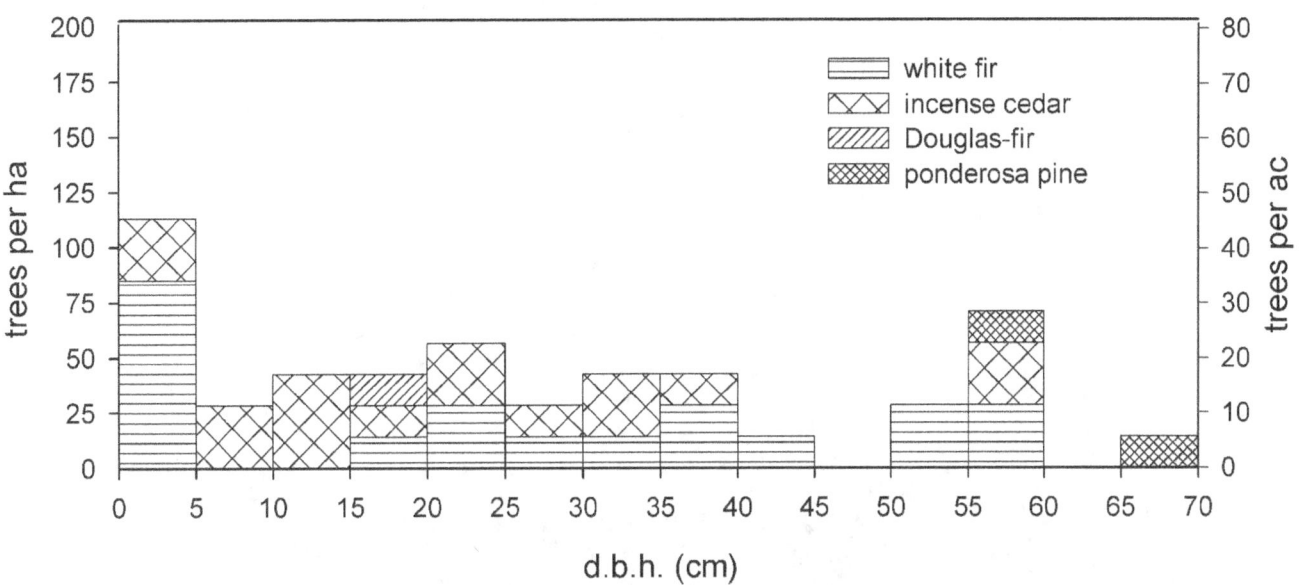

d.b.h. (cm)

Stand and canopy fuel data

	Units	White fir	Incense cedar	Douglas-fir	Ponderosa pine	All species
Stem density	trees/ha	170	170	14	28	382
(≥10 cm)	trees/acre	69	69	6	11	155
Basal area	m²/ha	22.8	14.8	0.4	8.9	46.8
	ft²/acre	99	64	2	39	204
Branch biomass	kg/m²	1.36	1.12	0.04	1.29	3.80
	tons/acre	6.06	5.00	0.16	5.74	16.97
Foliage biomass	kg/m²	0.65	0.46	0.02	0.35	1.48
	tons/acre	2.89	2.05	0.09	1.56	6.61
Bole biomass	kg/m²	9.91	3.54	0.09	5.07	18.61
	tons/acre	44.22	15.81	0.39	22.59	83.02
Total above-	kg/m²	11.92	5.13	0.14	6.70	23.89
ground biomass	tons/acre	53.17	22.89	0.64	29.90	106.59
Canopy fuel	kg/m²	0.81	0.53	0.02	0.35	1.72
load	tons/acre	3.61	2.37	0.11	1.56	7.66
Stand height	m					34
	ft					112
Canopy base	m					2
height	ft					7
Canopy fuel	kg/m³					0.101
bulk density	lbs/ft³					0.0063

Sierra Nevada mixed conifer
Understory removed (≤15 cm)

Stereo photo pair

Hemispherical photo

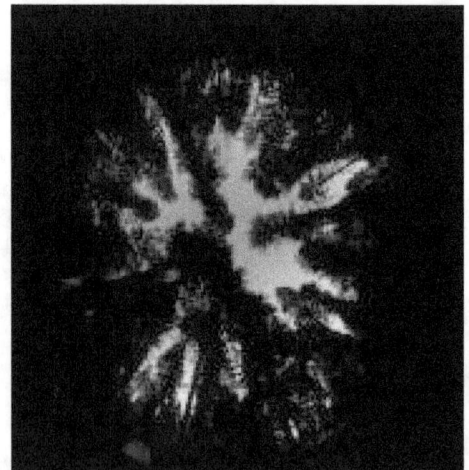

Gap fraction   0.26
Canopy cover (pct)   74

Canopy fuel profile

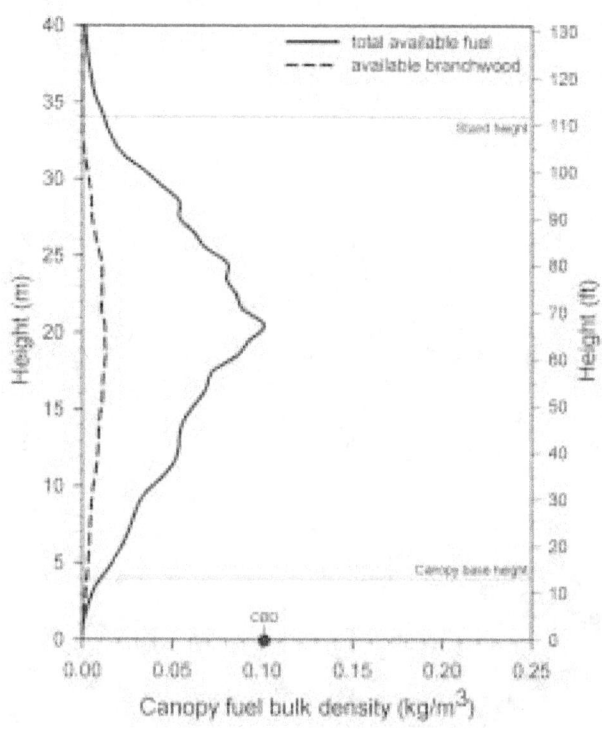

Stem diameter distribution

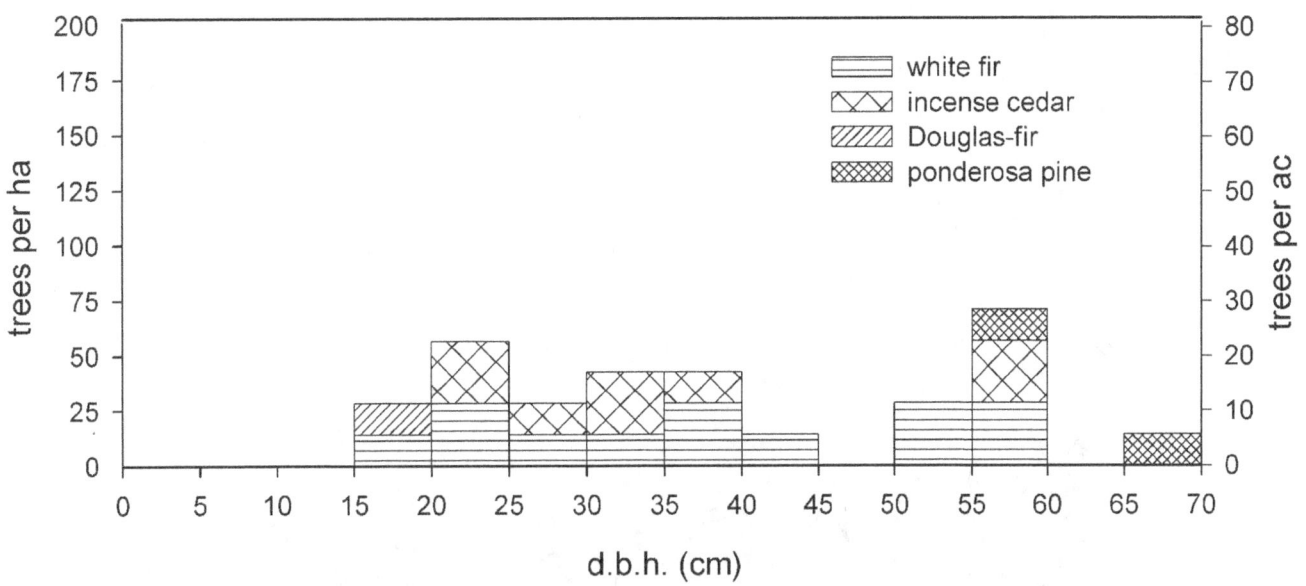

Stand and canopy fuel data

	Units	White fir	Incense cedar	Douglas-fir	Ponderosa pine	All species
Stem density	trees/ha	170	113	14	28	325
(≥10 cm)	trees/acre	69	46	6	11	132
Basal area	m²/ha	22.7	13.8	0.4	8.9	45.8
	ft²/acre	99	60	2	39	200
Branch biomass	kg/m²	1.35	1.08	0.04	1.29	3.75
	tons/acre	6.04	4.80	0.16	5.74	16.74
Foliage biomass	kg/m²	0.64	0.43	0.02	0.35	1.44
	tons/acre	2.87	1.92	0.09	1.56	6.44
Bole biomass	kg/m²	9.91	3.46	0.09	5.07	18.52
	tons/acre	44.21	15.42	0.39	22.59	82.61
Total above-ground biomass	kg/m²	11.91	4.96	0.14	6.70	23.75
	tons/acre	53.11	22.14	0.64	29.90	105.95
Canopy fuel load	kg/m²	0.80	0.49	0.02	0.35	1.67
	tons/acre	3.59	2.19	0.11	1.56	7.45
Stand height	m					34
	ft					112
Canopy base height	m					4
	ft					13
Canopy fuel bulk density	kg/m³					0.101
	lbs/ft³					0.0063

Sierra Nevada mixed conifer
75 percent of initial basal area

Stereo photo pair

Hemispherical photo

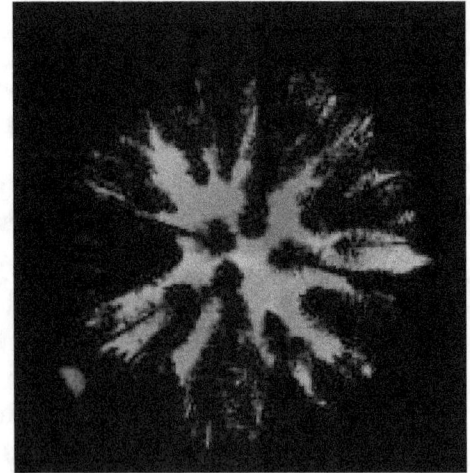

Gap fraction   0.40
Canopy cover (pct)   60

Canopy fuel profile

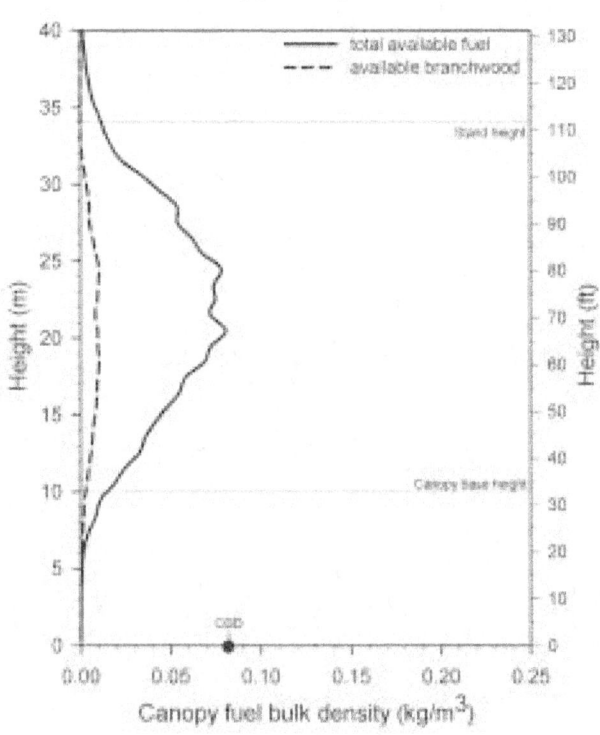

Stem diameter distribution

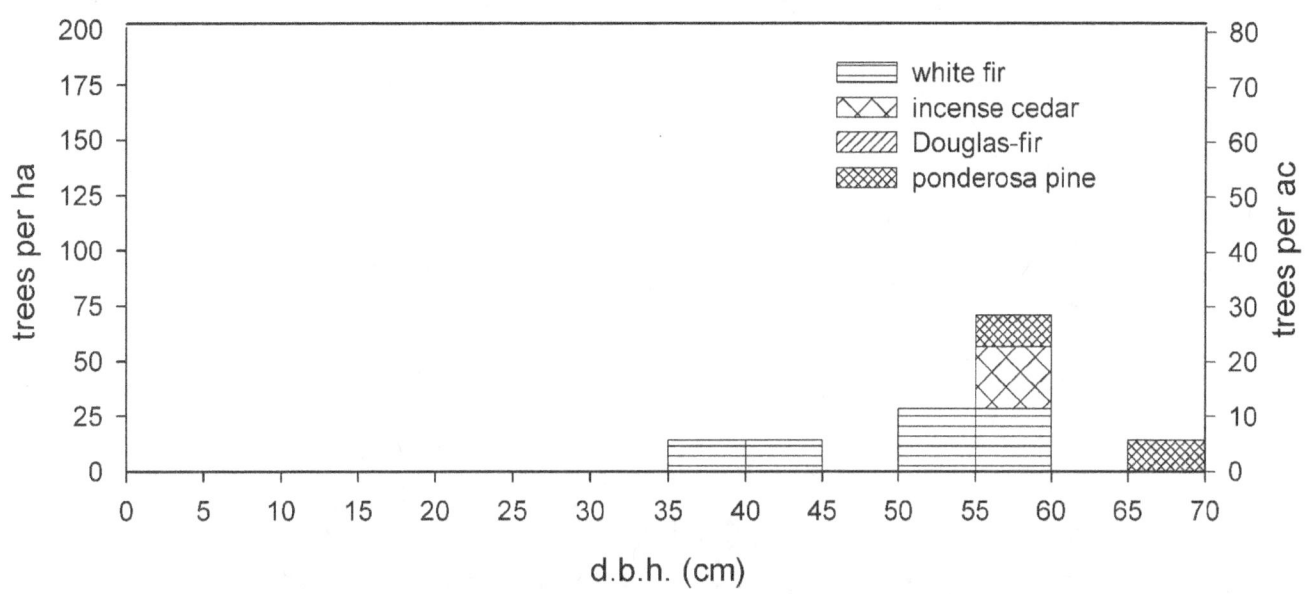

Stand and canopy fuel data

	Units	White fir	Incense cedar	Douglas-fir	Ponderosa pine	All species
Stem density	trees/ha	85	28	0	28	142
(≥10 cm)	trees/acre	34	11	0	11	57
Basal area	m²/ha	17.9	7.6	0.0	8.9	34.3
	ft²/acre	78	33	0	39	150
Branch biomass	kg/m²	1.16	0.62	0.00	1.29	3.07
	tons/acre	5.19	2.75	0.00	5.74	13.69
Foliage biomass	kg/m²	0.52	0.23	0.00	0.35	1.10
	tons/acre	2.31	1.04	0.00	1.56	4.92
Bole biomass	kg/m²	8.10	2.11	0.00	5.07	15.28
	tons/acre	36.14	9.42	0.00	22.59	68.16
Total above-	kg/m²	9.79	2.96	0.00	6.70	19.45
ground biomass	tons/acre	43.65	13.21	0.00	29.90	86.76
Canopy fuel	kg/m²	0.66	0.26	0.00	0.35	1.27
load	tons/acre	2.93	1.17	0.00	1.56	5.66
Stand height	m					34
	ft					112
Canopy base	m					10
height	ft					33
Canopy fuel	kg/m³					0.081
bulk density	lbs/ft³					0.0050

Sierra Nevada mixed conifer
50 percent of initial basal area

Stereo photo pair

Hemispherical photo

Gap fraction   0.56
Canopy cover (pct)   44

Canopy fuel profile

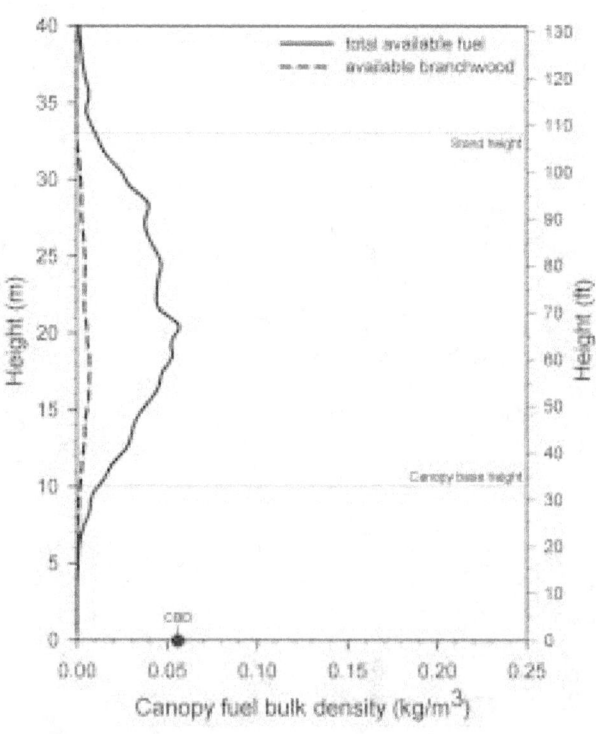

Stem diameter distribution

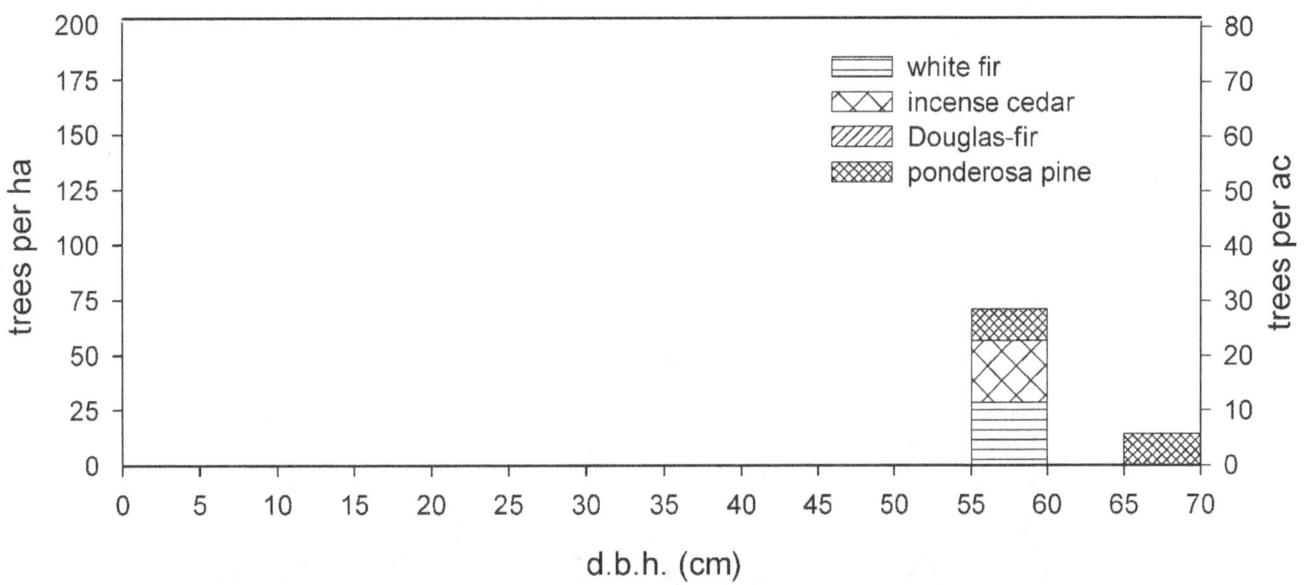

Stand and canopy fuel data

	Units	White fir	Incense cedar	Douglas-fir	Ponderosa pine	All species
Stem density	trees/ha	28	28	0	28	85
(≥10 cm)	trees/acre	11	11	0	11	34
Basal area	m²/ha	7.7	7.6	0.0	8.9	24.2
	ft²/acre	33	33	0	39	105
Branch biomass	kg/m²	0.61	0.62	0.00	1.29	2.52
	tons/acre	2.74	2.75	0.00	5.74	11.23
Foliage biomass	kg/m²	0.25	0.23	0.00	0.35	0.84
	tons/acre	1.13	1.04	0.00	1.56	3.73
Bole biomass	kg/m²	3.19	2.11	0.00	5.07	10.37
	tons/acre	14.24	9.41	0.00	22.59	46.25
Total above-ground biomass	kg/m²	4.06	2.96	0.00	6.70	13.72
	tons/acre	18.10	13.21	0.00	29.90	61.21
Canopy fuel load	kg/m²	0.32	0.26	0.00	0.35	0.93
	tons/acre	1.43	1.17	0.00	1.56	4.17
Stand height	m					33
	ft					108
Canopy base height	m					11
	ft					36
Canopy fuel bulk density	kg/m³					0.037
	lbs/ft³					0.0023

Sierra Nevada mixed conifer
25 percent of initial basal area

Stereo photo pair

Hemispherical photo

Gap fraction   0.73
Canopy cover (pct)   27

Canopy fuel profile

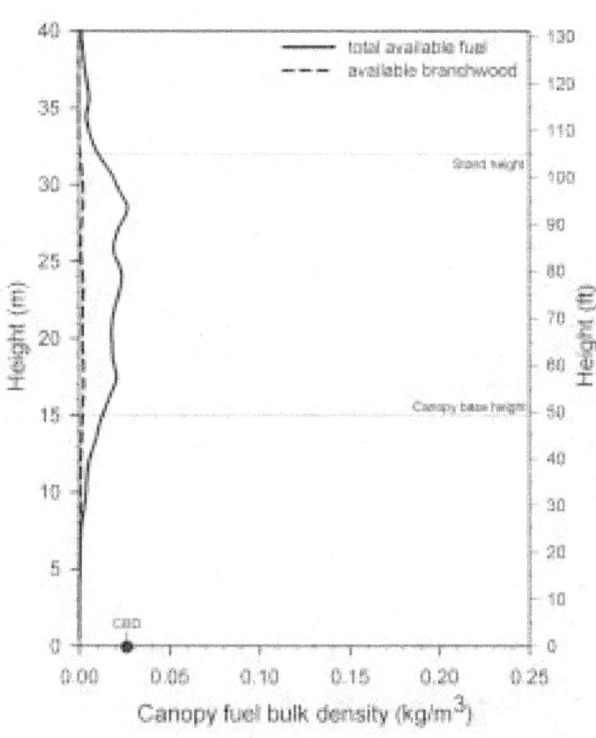

Stem diameter distribution

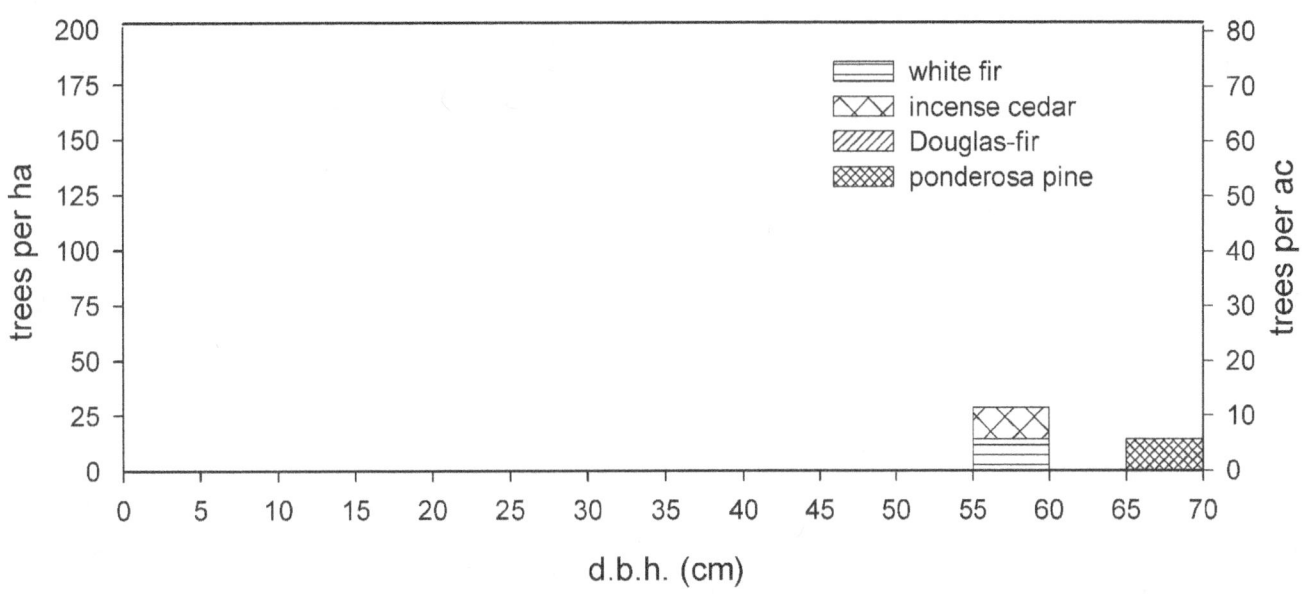

Stand and canopy fuel data

	Units	White fir	Incense cedar	Douglas-fir	Ponderosa pine	All species
Stem density	trees/ha	14	14	0	14	42
(≥10 cm)	trees/acre	6	6	0	6	17
Basal area	m²/ha	3.9	3.9	0.0	5.0	12.7
	ft²/acre	17	17	0	22	55
Branch biomass	kg/m²	0.28	0.26	0.00	0.68	1.22
	tons/acre	1.24	1.17	0.00	3.04	5.45
Foliage biomass	kg/m²	0.11	0.10	0.00	0.18	0.40
	tons/acre	0.50	0.44	0.00	0.82	1.77
Bole biomass	kg/m²	1.49	1.17	0.00	2.79	5.44
	tons/acre	6.65	5.20	0.00	12.43	24.28
Total above-ground biomass	kg/m²	1.88	1.53	0.00	3.65	7.06
	tons/acre	8.39	6.82	0.00	16.29	31.50
Canopy fuel load	kg/m²	0.14	0.11	0.00	0.18	0.44
	tons/acre	0.64	0.50	0.00	0.82	1.97
Stand height	m					32
	ft					105
Canopy base height	m					15
	ft					49
Canopy fuel bulk density	kg/m³					0.027
	lbs/ft³					0.0017

Notes